An Emerald Earth

To Qahira and Shane,

For two protectors of
the Emerald Earth, with
Love and Appreciation
Sharifa & Menmuchin

This book belongs to

David Johnson
5787 Barnes Rd.
Canandaigua, NY 14424

AN EMERALD EARTH

CULTIVATING A NATURAL SPIRITUALITY AND SERVING CREATIVE BEAUTY IN OUR WORLD

Felicia Norton and Charles Smith, PhD

TWO SEAS JOIN PRESS

NEW YORK

WWW.TWOSEASJOIN.ORG

First published in the United States in 2008 by
TwoSeasJoin Press, 235 E. 22nd St. #2V, New York, NY 10010

Printed in the United States.

Library of Congress Control Number: 2008907009

ISBN 978-0-6152-3546-2

Quote of Hazrat Inayat Khan on page v from *The Way of Illumination*,
(Geneva: International Sufi Movement, 1960), p. 15.

Quotes of Master Dogen on page v from *The True Dharma Eye, Zen Master
Dogen's Three Hundred Koans*, translated by Kazuaki Tanahashi and John
Daido Loori (Boston: Shambhala Publications, 2005), p. 22.

Credits: Photos on pages 8, 45 and 140, Katrina Belanger-Smith; page 16,
Office of His Eminence Jamgon Kongtrul Rinpoche. Other photos, layout
and cover design by Charles Smith.

The Hope Project (see picture caption on page 24) is a registered charitable
trust, founded in 1980 by the Sufi teacher Pir Vilayat Inayat Khan. Moved
by the extreme poverty of the people living in the Nizamuddin area of
Delhi, India, Pir Vilayat initiated a program that would enable the poor
to help themselves. The Hope Project runs a community health center,
a school, vocational training courses, a credit program for starting small
businesses and a women's cooperative enterprise. For more information
on the Hope Project see http://www.hopeprojectindia.org/.

A portion of the proceeds from the sale of this book are donated to not-
for-profit organizations working for humanitarian relief
and for the restoration of the natural environment.

Sunrise in the Yellow Mountains, China

There is One Holy Book, the sacred manuscript of nature, the only scripture which can enlighten the reader.

—Hazrat Inayat Khan

Zen master Jingcen of Changsha was once asked by a monastic, "How do you turn the mountains, rivers and great earth and return to the self?"

Changsha said, "How do you turn the self and return to the mountains, rivers and great earth?"

—Master Dogen

Dedicated to Pir Vilayat Inayat Khan (1916-2004), the son of the great Indian mystic Hazrat Inayat Khan. Pir Vilayat carried his father's expansive vision of spirituality into the present age, teaching and guiding many thousands of Westerners from the 1960s until his passing in 2004. Pir Vilayat's teachings bring to light a universal spirituality, rooted in service, joy and creativity, and leading towards the one boundless and embracing Reality, the perfection of love, harmony and beauty.

We offer our deepest gratitude to our families and friends, and to our spiritual guides, especially Zia Inayat Khan, Aziza and Akbar Scott, Shahabuddin Less, Fariha-al-Jerrahi, James Parks Morton and Lama Norhla Rinpoche.

We are especially grateful to Sarah Gallogly for her fine editorial work and helpful suggestions.

TABLE OF CONTENTS

PROLOGUE: HOME TO AN EMERALD EARTH   ix

PART I: AWAKENING TO AN EMERALD EARTH   1
   1   THE CALL OF REALITY   3
   2   AWAKENING TO FREEDOM   6
   3   GUIDANCE AWAITS US   9
   4   THE NATURAL STATE   16
   5   RECEIVING THE MAGICAL PALACE   19
   6   OUR TRUE BEING IS HAPPINESS   24
   7   EVERY MOVEMENT IS A MOVEMENT OF LOVE   26
   8   THE MONASTERY OF THE WORLD   28
   9   THE BELOVED INVITES US ALL   31

PART II: PREPARING THE FIELD   34
   10   THE OPENING OF THE WAY   37
   11   IN THE DARKNESS BEYOND REASON: KALI'S PLAY   40
   12   THE CURE IN THE PAIN   43
   13   VULNERABILITY   46
   14   ON BEING TESTED   48
   15   ENTERING THE STREAM   52
   16   THE HEART'S NATURAL PITCH   55
   17   WORKING WITH IMPRESSIONS   58
   18   SPIRITUAL PRACTICES AS HELPFUL FRIENDS   61

INTRODUCTION TO PRACTICES   63

PRACTICES — PREPARING THE FIELD OF THE HEART   66
   Practice #1: Tranquility Meditation   66
   Practice #2: Elemental Purification Breaths   68
   Practice #3: Working with Light   74
   Practice #4: Facing a Bright Window   76
   Practice #5: Tuning the Heart   77
   Practice #6: Mystic Concentration   79
   Practice #7: A Breathing Practice for Deep Concentration   81
   Practice #8: Becoming Transparent to Light   82

PART III: TOUCHING THE GROUND OF BEING   84
   19   THE ESSENCE OF BEING   85
   20   REDISCOVERING INNER SENSES   87
   21   THE BACKWARD STEP   89

PRACTICES—TOUCHING THE GROUND OF BEING 91
  Practice #9: Progressive Relaxation 91
  Practice #10: Insight Meditation 93
  Practice #11: Uncreated Light 97
  Practice #12: Light upon a Light 97

PART IV: SOWING THE SEEDS OF AN EMERALD EARTH 99
  22 ON SOWING AND BEING SOWN 101
  23 THE HIDDEN TREASURE 103
  24 THE YEAST OF A NEW CREATION 105

PRACTICES—SOWING SEEDS OF AN EMERALD EARTH 107
  Practice #13: Walking Bodhisattva Meditation 107
  Practice #14: Creative Imagination Practice 109
  Practice #15: The Use of A Sacred Name or Mantra 110
  Practice #16: The Journey of Love 112

PART V: THE HARVEST—REALIZING AN EMERALD EARTH 115
  25 THE GREAT WORK 117
  26 THE CHILD OF THE MOMENT 120
  27 AWAKENING IN LIFE 122
  28 THE PURPOSE OF LIFE 126
  29 THE MUSIC OF LIFE 129
  30 TO DANCE AT THE COURT OF INDRA 131
  31 A TABLE SPREAD 133
  32 SERVING THE GUESTS 136
  33 SHARING THE GIFT OF AWAKENING 138
  34 THE SURVIVAL ARK 140
  35 A UNIVERSE SEEKING BEAUTY 144
  36 CREATIVE BEAUTY—THE WAY OF SOPHIA 146

PRACTICES—THE HARVEST 149
  Practice #17: Concentration Practice: Life Energy 149
  Practice #18: Newly Emerging Buds Of Potential 151
  Practice #19: Meditation on the Shekinah 153
  Practice #20: Reading Nature's Manuscript 155
  Practice #21: The Fulfillment of the Soul's Desire 156
  Practice #22: Nourishing the Field of Our Being 159
  Practice #23: True Vision- The Creative Glance 162
  Practice #24: Fruitfulness 166

EPILOGUE: AN ELIXIR FOR HUMANITY 168

PROLOGUE:
HOME TO AN EMERALD EARTH

This groggy time we live,
this is what it's like:
A man goes to sleep in the town
where he has always lived,
and he dreams he's living in another town.
In the dream, he doesn't remember
the town he's sleeping in his bed in.
He believes the reality of the dream town.

The world is that kind of sleep.
The dust of many crumbled cities
settles over us like a forgetful daze.
We are older than those cities.
We began as a mineral.
We emerged into plant life
and moved into the animal state,
and then into being human,
and always we have forgotten our former states,
except in early spring when we
slightly recall being green again.

Humankind is being led along an evolving course,
through this migration of intelligences,
and though we seem to be sleeping,
there is an inner wakefulness
that directs the dream,
and that will eventually startle us back
to the truth of who we are.[1]

THE EMERALD SPEAKS OF NEW LIFE, BEAUTY AND WISDOM. Ancient lore describes how Universal Spirit, as a Primordial Intelligence, wished to experience life, but needed a mirror. The emerald is symbolic of this mirror, the Universal Soul who offers Herself as the very form which will be shaped, "written upon", and brought forth as creation. The emerald's deep and clear green color, uplifting and strengthening to our spirits, is a testimony to the truth that beauty and

[1] Jelaluddin Rumi, *The Essential Rumi*, trans. Coleman Barks (San Francisco: Harper Collins, 1995), pp. 112–13.

clarity can arise from the depths of matter. The life-giving emerald color emerges from joining equal parts of an earthly yellow and a heavenly blue, the marriage of heaven and earth. It evokes, most spontaneously, appreciation for the beauty, richness and enchantment of this life. The emerald speaks directly to us of the exquisite beauty that emerges from the heat, pressure and duration of its embodiment in matter.

Sufi master Hazrat Inayat Khan taught that contemplating an emerald encouraged creative opening and forward movement in the human being. Speaking to the infinite power and divine knowledge that is hidden in our hearts, the emerald evokes our deepest desires to see and move beyond mundane perception, and to bring forth new worlds, both within and without.

The emerald is also described in the Sufi tradition as the gem that helps us to "remember" something long forgotten and crucial: the essential purpose of our lives. In related Persian lore, an emerald mountain symbolizes *a place of return* where the soul remembers its source and regains awareness of an archetypal world of "true imagination." This world is alternatively referred to as the "place" where inner and outer realities meet, where "the two seas join." As we will explore below, this "place" presents guidance that is bewildering to our ordinary thinking but that ultimately transforms and clarifies our vision of Reality. Paralleling this lore is *The Emerald Tablet*, ascribed to the ancient sage Hermes, a guidebook for finding the "philosopher's stone," the secret of eternal life. The *Emerald Tablet* begins by affirming the vital interdependence of heaven and earth: "*The above from the below, and the below from the above—the work of the miracle of the One*".

As inheritors of all of the planes of creation, we experience and carry forward, in our bodies, hearts and souls, the evolutionary intelligence and wisdom of all ages. In our lives we can choose to consciously affirm and safeguard this inheritance by realizing we live within a sacred and miraculous world. To the degree we do this, we bring forth an Emerald Earth—all of life becomes a living expression of Universal Soul, reflecting beauty and wisdom, serving and cultivating an uplifted humanity. In turn, bringing forth an Emerald Earth fulfills the very impulse behind life, yielding true freedom and the deepest satisfaction a human being could attain.

We invoke an image of an Emerald Earth as the expression of our deepest desire to know and live closely to a world of beauty and harmony, the world of the Universal Soul. This is a choice, and we emphasize that it is one that is absolutely vital for the life around us. In the words of Dostoevsky, "only beauty will save the world." The affirmation of a world of beauty—the bringing forth of an Emerald Earth—relates directly to what Thomas Berry identified as the "Great Work" of our age,[2] the safeguarding and restoration of our natural world. Without this vital work, we may not continue our existence on this planet. This work must begin inside of us, because our psyches, like our rivers and seas, are polluted. Until we truly heal and restore ourselves, we will continue, even with the best of intentions, to damage the life around us.

Sages since antiquity have taught that all wisdom is within us, waiting to be unveiled. In our bodies, minds and souls we share an identity with the whole of existence. For ages we have entertained a radical separation of matter and spirit, and of Divine and human. Now, our survival hinges on overcoming this separation and attaining a condition in which the spiritual and material are honored and can work in harmony. For this to be possible, we must explore simultaneously within and without, reading nature's sacred manuscript with a vision that is illuminated by the soul. By this we can be guided toward most precise and elegantly ways to cultivate, embody and protect the beauty of the natural world and each moment of life.

Nature speaks to us directly. The rocks and trees, the beautiful and delicate flowers, the expanse of the sky, the power and truth of thunder and lightning, and the wisdom of still mountains and flowing rivers are living scriptures speaking to us. Nature asks us to step back from the confusion all around us and appreciate Her life-giving sanity and way of teaching. She call us home to the realization that we are not separate spectators:

> *Mountains, rivers and the great earth are ceaselessly manifesting the teachings, yet they are not heard with the ear or seen with the eye. They can only be perceived with the whole body and mind. Be that as it may, how do you turn the self and return to the mountains, rivers and great earth? What is it that you are calling mountains, rivers and the great earth? Indeed, where do you find yourself?[3].*

---

[2] See Thomas Berry, *The Great Work: Our Way into the Future* (New York: Harmony Bell Tower, 2000). Berry contrasts the present challenge of stewardship of the Earth with the "Great Work" of the past, the latter a focus on individual spiritual transformation.

[3] Master Dogen, in *The True Dharma Eye, Zen Master Dogen's Three Hundred Koans*, trans. Kazuaki Tanahashi and John Daido Loori (Boston: Shambhala, 2005), p. 22.

Like the gem, an Emerald Earth is self-revealing of a state of upliftment, of remembrance, of progression towards greater beauty and more intelligent ways of living. It calls us to a sacred and awesome work, one that will take us far beyond conventional forms of meditation and spirituality. This "Great Work" promises to bring us to a most intimate and fulfilling relationship with all of life.

The challenge of realizing an Emerald Earth calls us to radically embrace an expanded view of what is possible in this world. To gain and then maintain this view, we describe here the sacred work of return, of polishing and cultivating the heart, of bringing forth our inherent joy and satisfaction within the precious moments of our earthly sojourn. We emphasize the importance of knowing abundance and generosity in our lives, and of being able to offer these to others. We affirm the need to all make concerted efforts to move beyond our selfishness without sacrificing our uniqueness. We must learn to honor our desires but challenge our tendencies towards greed, and seek wisdom and meaning in each moment. We must call on courage to face pain, to heal ourselves and to embrace the sacred light within us.

The present age calls us, urges us to bring the light of our souls to bear on every aspect of existence. In the same way as it has inspired great advances in humanity in the past, the vision resulting from this light is crucial for bringing to fruition the many positive environmental and social advances that are emerging all around us. The words of Muinuddin Chishti, a revered thirteenth-century Sufi and great humanitarian, provide us with both a caution and a sound basis for our movement towards a better world:

> *Love all and hate none. Mere talk of peace will avail you naught.*
> *Mere talk of God and religion will not take you far.*
> *Bring out all of the latent powers of your being*
> *and reveal the full magnificence of your immortal "self."*
> *Be surcharged with peace and joy,*
> *and scatter these wherever you are and wherever you go.*
> *Be a blazing fire of Truth, be a beauteous blossom of love,*
> *and be a soothing balm of peace.*
> *With your spiritual light, dispel the darkness of ignorance;*
> *Dissolve the clouds of discord and war and spread goodwill,*
> *peace and harmony among the people.*[4]

---

[4] Hazrat Muinuddin Chishti, in William Begg, *The Holy Biography of Hazrat Khwaja Muinuddin Chishti* (The Hague: East-West Publications, 1977), p. 12.

The Language of Cultivation

Pir Vilayat Khan, a pioneer of consciousness in this age, posed critical questions to the seeker of wisdom. "What if your picture of the universe is not the universe at all? What if nature is truly a living sacred manuscript, offering you moment-to-moment signs and symbols, the language of a far greater Reality? And what if this life is a malleable and workable dream, which can be shaped, restored, and beautified by our intentions and actions?"

True spirituality can be known, as Christ said, by its fruits. It is in our hands to use spiritual principles to change the dreamscape of this life, to bring forth an uplifted world. True spirituality should enable us to move away from narrow interpretations of Reality that damage our environment and threaten the continuity of life as we know it. By the very fact that the dream reality we live in is malleable, we cannot afford to believe ourselves puppets on a string, moved about by fixed definitions of God, chance or destiny. The hope for our world is belief in our power to make a difference, not by grandiose programs but in the day-to-day ecology that begins in our own minds and hearts.

Beneath the endless distractions of life there is a treasure, a living grain that can become a magnificent flower or tree. The treasure within us exists not only for us but for the whole of life. Every struggle, every deep issue that we work out in ourselves reveals more of this treasure and ultimately bears fruit for all.

There are stories in the Tibetan tradition of how certain dakinis, feminine deities and protectors of the sacred, will grind gems, pulverize them and feed the Earth with them. This symbolizes the enrichment that happens when we set about the "Great Work" dedicated to all, affirming and protecting the beauty of the Emerald Earth. We dig and mine the infinite storehouse of jewels within us for ourselves and our world.

To express the ancient wisdom that helps us know and honor the cultivation of our being, this book will use many images from nature, especially from the garden and the farm. Seeds, plants, trees and fruit speak for themselves; as natural symbols they are immediately and intuitively understandable. Perhaps for this reason nature's language has been used since antiquity to describe human transformation.

The word alchemy, so often applied to such transformation, is from the Arabic, *Al Kima*, literally meaning "black earth" and referring to the fertile land of Egypt, from which the ancient art is thought to have come. This reference seems more than coincidental, given the great spiritual teachings that urge us to make our beings into fertile fields.[5]

Just as in the cultivation of the field, the soil of our hearts must be turned and turned, made soft and free from rocks and pebbles before seeds are planted. Like a plant or tree, we must open to the elements —to the waters, air, light and substance we need to naturally unfold, grow and bear abundant flowers and fruits. The meaning here is both metaphorical and literal. We open also to plowing and harrowing, loosening stones and pebbles from our minds and hearts, removing all obstacles that prevent new seeds from sprouting and growing. Sometimes we are sowing seeds by our thoughts and actions, bringing light and possibility to the field. To insure a bountiful and beautiful harvest for all of life, we must continually uproot what Buddha called the "weeds of illusion" in ourselves and the world around us. By this we insure a bountiful and beautiful harvest for all of life.

True spirituality is a completely natural movement towards sanity, towards our natural state. It means, quite literally, coming to our senses. It means attaining an awe and reverence for the magic and mystery in life and for the power and beauty of nature. It is not an arrival at a final destination, but simply a state of openness to an ongoing action of transformation. It means a greater acceptance of raw pain, of the fullness of joy, of moments of stark emptiness, of radiant blossoming, of floods and dry spells and of verdant fields and fragrant gardens.

Dedication

We have dedicated this book to our meditation teacher, Pir Vilayat Khan, who often used the metaphors of agriculture and alchemy side by side with the language of modern science. Like his father, Hazrat Inayat Khan, Pir Vilayat saw that the spirituality of this age must depart radically from the ways of the past, that dogma and ritual must give way to dialogue and understanding. He felt strongly that science and spirituality could enter into dialogue and work together to guide humanity. Awarded the Juliet Hollister Award for interfaith

---

[5] As Jung noted, the alchemist's descriptions of "alchemical operations" left us with most profound images of change and transformation processes. These descriptions are being recognized anew via emerging paradigms of science. See pages 35-37 below.

understanding, Pir Vilayat devoted his life to helping humanity to capture the essence of spiritual realization and apply it to everyday life, thereby wisely and compassionately addressing the problems around us.

When we realize we have been asleep to our deepest identity, and that our life is a malleable dream, we become much more effective in helping ourselves and contributing to the life around us. Without being completely overwhelmed by life's intensity, we can fulfill our potential. Instead of reacting out of stress or fear, we can act creatively and effectively. Our situations become workable, and our life becomes a most fertile field, yielding precious flowers, fruits and grains not only for ourselves but for all. Rather than being an escape from difficulty, meditation becomes a tool for fulfilling our unique role within life.

With awakening consciousness we realize together that we are the living embodiment of an unfathomably great mystery. We come to see our life as the continual effusion of an All-Possible universe, a mystery that is continually calling us into Being. Universal Consciousness becomes localized within us: this extraordinary mystery, filled with freedom and possibility, presents itself anew in each moment within our hearts.

May we share the joy of awakening to an intimacy with this Mystery, realizing it as pure affirmation of our being and as ultimate abundance and satisfaction. May we discover and unfold the infinitude of treasures coming from our depths. May compassion guide us, and may we realize the profound benefits for our world that come through each step we take on the path of awakening. And may we participate fully in nature's passion for bringing forth beauty, within us and in the world around us.

Felicia Norton and Charles Smith
New York City, July 5, 2008

PART I: Awakening to an Emerald Earth

Part I of this book offers a first glimpse of an Emerald Earth. It is an invitation to take a step towards greater realization of the deeper reality that is ever seeking to inform our lives.

Introduction: Kindled In Glory

Beloved, Thou makest me fuller every day.
Thou diggest into my heart deeper than the depths of the earth.
Thou raisest my soul higher than the highest heaven,
making me more empty every day and yet fuller.
Thou makest me wider than the ends of the world;
Thou stretchest my two arms across the land and the sea,
giving into my enfoldment the East and the West.
Thou changest my flesh into fertile soil;
Thou turnest my blood into streams of water;
Thou kneadest my clay, I know,
to make a new universe.[6]

MANY SPIRITUAL TRADITIONS SHARE A STORY about a moment before creation in which our souls were kindled in an act of glory. In that moment we were asked if we would pledge, while on Earth, to uphold the sacred, to remember and celebrate the splendor and beauty of the Unseen Mystery from which we come. Some accounts relate that we resisted coming here, fearful of all the difficulties that the earthly journey would involve. It is said that the Divine had to play beautiful music to entice our souls. Hearing the music and moved to ecstasy, we danced into our earthly bodies.

Somewhere in our depths, we carry a faint memory of this pledge, now reflected in our deep desire for a meaningful life. But today we are too often distracted from the sacred, and from the beauty that we came here to celebrate.

Our happiness depends on remembering why we are here. Touching upon our nostalgia for beauty, celebration and meaning opens a door to Reality. In turn, Reality guides us home, not to hidden and esoteric mysteries but to our most essential and natural self, our joy and fulfillment.

[6] Hazrat Inayat Khan, *Complete Sayings, Vadan* (New Lebanon, NY: Sufi Order Publications, 1978), p. 100.

1

Coming home to our own depths can feel frightening, but it is the way to our greatest happiness and freedom. In truth, fulfilling our long-forgotten covenant with the Universe is the key to lifting the illusory burden of our lives. A dedication to accenting and serving the sacred opens a door to the ease, peace and harmony at our core of our being.

At the same time, an authentic spiritual journey opens us more fully to pain, and cannot help but take us though intense experiences. The fullness of our spiritual awakening leaves no stone unturned, and makes us aware of every obstacle to our happiness and fulfillment.

However intense our awakening must be, our soul has been awaiting this crucial dawning since before time. There is an exciting challenge in seeking the sacred in the everyday world, of being fully involved in life while at the same time being in touch with the soul's natural state of happiness and freedom. It is by this alchemy that the fullness, beauty and potential of our life are realized, and we truly find ourselves at home on an Emerald Earth.

The One who floods the private sanctuary I have built.
The One who takes away sleep,
who drags and throws me under,
that presence is the joy I speak.[7]

[7] Jelaluddin Rumi, in *Unseen Rain,* trans. John Moyne and Coleman Barks, (Putney, VT: Threshold Books), p. 1.

1
THE CALL OF REALITY

The sky is the azure salver,
the sun and moon are Thy lamps.
The stars are Thy scattered pearls,
the sandal forests are Thy incense,
and the breeze is Thy fan.
What other worship can be compared
To Nature's own festival of lights?
I'm enchanted with Thy play.
It is the light
which lives in every heart,
and Thy light
which illumines every soul.[8]

WISDOM IS EVER CALLING TO us. She calls through Her beauty, through the vast expanse of the galaxies in the night sky, through the sun and moon as they rise and adorn fields and cities. She speaks in the wonder of children, through the mind of great thinkers, through our moments of conflict and confusion, and through our worst mistakes.

Wisdom speaks most clearly through our most ordinary human experience, our joy and expansiveness, our pain and losses. She calls and offers us an opportunity to play our part in restoring and transforming ourselves and the life around us.

To learn something new, or to see our life through different eyes, we have to forge new pathways, both metaphorically and physiologically. The mind is deeply conditioned to be comfortable with its familiar and yet imprisoning routines, running mechanically along lines of thought that it knows well. It resists and sometimes avoids new pathways of fresh, original thinking, however liberating these may be.

Wisdom's call is to affirm a world of beauty, an Emerald Earth. This challenging course requires no less than a new way of seeing and of meeting life. New ways of seeing and thinking, even in bringing freedom, are painful to contemplate and to realize. As Plato described our predicament, we are chained in a cave, and only the courageous

---

[8] Sikh Scriptures, *Guru Granth Sahib*. This is part of the *Rag Dhanasari*, a song by Guru Nanak, the first of the Sikh Gurus. The translation is from *Peace Lagoon*, compiled by Sardarni Premka Kaur (Espanola, NM: Sikh Dharma, 2004), p. 179.

will step outside of ordinary consciousness and encounter "Reality." Coming back to relate what they have seen, these explorers are met with scorn and suspicion.

What makes the encounter with Reality even more challenging is the radical unlearning it requires of us. Unlearning is critical for two reasons. To understand the first reason we can reflect on the words in the Bible, "Lo, I make all things new." In the thought of the thirteenth-century Sufi Ibn Arabi, in every moment the universe appears in a "new configuration."[9] Some physicists today affirm this to be literally true: in each moment, the universe is switching on and off, dying and being reborn. This means that our knowledge of the workings of our universe and ourselves should be continually updated with new information. Given this situation, the true scientist must eventually come to a state of awe and bewilderment at all that remains unexplored or beyond our comprehension.

Henry Corbin's book *Spiritual Body and Celestial Earth* helps us understand the second main reason for unlearning. Corbin describes a cryptic Sufi teaching: that "in the whole of the universes of this Earth of Truth, for each soul a universe corresponding to that soul has been created." This means that there is no prescription for wisdom that applies to every person, and that, instead of a collective religion for all, each soul has its *own* religion, its own particular way of approaching and embracing truth. Each of us experiences Reality in a special and unique way. Seen from another angle, we could say that Reality is afforded many lenses by which it takes in the richness of life. When we are guided to and trusting in our unique way, our "soul's religion," the full splendor and mystery of existence has an opportunity to reveal itself.

In accord with Corbin's thought, we will describe the soul's Emerald Earth not as a life of transcendent or heavenly states, nor as existing only in the mind of a visionary mystic. Instead, it is a life emerging out of a deep intimacy with our own soul, fueled by the creative spark and passion of our being.

The Emerald Earth is a world animated by nature's imagination. It is awesome and vast, teeming with its own music, guiding all who

---

[9] In the words of Muhyiuddin Ibn Arabi, "Man does not know that he ceases to exist and then comes into existence again with every single breath." In Toshihiko Izutsu, *Sufism and Taoism* (Berkeley: University of California Press, 1984), see especially p. 205 and p. 211.

open to its loving arms. It is created by a play of the elements: of earth, water, fire, air and ether coming together, in service to life's Mystery. It is the play of nature within and around us—rains and storms, sun and clouds, thunder and lightning, times of fruitfulness and beauty. All that happens is a most exquisite choreography, every situation elegantly orchestrated to bring forth beauty.

To unlearn and gain the vision of an Emerald Earth, we must become free from the tyranny of the impressions and ever-jarring effects of the life around us. We must regain a capacity we had as children, well described by the psychologist Erik Erikson: "There is in every child, in every moment, a miracle unfolding." As adults, we can regain this capacity only by a great deal of inner work, a removal of those habitual lines of thinking that keep us from our most natural condition.

Sufi teachers speak of this work as the polishing of the mirror of the heart, whereby we remove all that keeps us from a natural sense of well-being. It is this polishing that begins a journey of natural spirituality, a journey of return to our most essential and intimate identity. In turn, this journey yields a clarity, spaciousness and sense of possibility in our being, allowing us to recognize an ever-renewing creation, an Emerald Earth.

2
AWAKENING TO FREEDOM

[Awakening] is like a person who admired a theatrical performance and found out how different everything was next morning. On awakening to the day, how different the view of the world becomes! Before the awakening, we with little knowledge think we know so much, but now our pride is broken. We find that all we had known hitherto is useless, that we have to begin all over again.[10]

LIVING WITH A TRANSFORMED VISION is a work of freeing ourselves, of uprooting old ways of thinking and acting. It is this work that brings us face to face with a life that is fresh, continually creative and ever filled with beauty and possibility.

Even with the knowledge that change is needed, negative conditions and stress easily hold sway over our consciousness. If we are sensitive beings, we feel deeply the pressure of earthly existence, the competitive struggle, the self-serving tactics and hypocrisy that cause people to lose their souls over things of little value. We see a world that is destroying itself through narrow thinking, insane religious and cultural clashes, greed and fear. Somehow, because we are connected to all beings, we feel deeply the pain and the burden of responsibility for a world gone amok.

For a solution, we must turn in a different direction. The Tibetan teacher Kalu Rinpoche provides a hint, explaining that the word for Buddha in Tibetan is *sangye*, which means "pure blooming."[11] When we are fully awake in a spiritual sense, even within the most negative conditions we feel ourselves to be in touch with an inner sense of blossoming and purity. Seeing life the way that the Buddha did, we realize that the only solution to the problems around us begins within our own being. Our most positive, life-giving thoughts can, when backed by deep and strongly concentration, affect the life around

[10] Hazrat Inayat Khan, *The Sufi Message of Hazrat Inayat Khan,* Vol. XII: The Vision of God in Man, (Geneva: International Sufi Movement, 1982), p. 65

[11] Kalu Rinpoche, *Secret Buddhism* (San Francisco: Clear Point Press, 1995), p. 120.

us, counterbalancing the negative thinking that otherwise tends to prevail.

Giving positive direction to our thinking is an invaluable stepping stone, crucial to a healthy and happy life. Yet spiritual practices, such as will be described here, will allow us to work at a deeper level. Developing relaxation, clarity of the mind, awareness of great spaciousness and inner strength help us to touch the root of problems. The realization that practices bring allows us, even in the most difficult circumstances, to bring forth understanding, clarity, wisdom and creativity—to know and live from a place of "pure blooming," and to bring this to each moment.

A Universe of All Possibility

There is a difficulty in naming the Divine Mystery we live within. The name "God" seems to place the Divine far outside of us. Hazrat Inayat Khan preferred to accent the compassionate and loving nature of the universe through the name the "All-Possible." He used the story of Kalpavriksha, a "wish-fulfilling tree" to describe this attribute. This magical tree, so the story goes, grants the sincere wishes of all who sit beneath it. A man, upon hearing of its power, approached the tree and sat down underneath it. He asked for pears and, indeed, pears appeared. When he wished for roses, vibrant and beautiful rose blossoms appeared before his eyes. Then, in a moment of doubt, the man thought that the Kalpavriksha must be his imagination. In an instant, the tree disappeared. In Inayat Khan's words:

> *For this tree is this whole universe, the miniature of which is one's own self, and there is nothing that you ask that this universe will not answer, for it is the nature of the universe to answer your soul's call. Only, if you ask for the pears, there are pears... if you ask for the rose there will be the rose and its thorns together. And it is the lack of knowledge of this great secret hidden in the heart of the universe which is the only tragedy of life. When a person seeks for something in the universe and he cannot find it, it is not true that it is not there, the fact is that he does not see it.* [12]

The existence of this wish-fulfilling tree is an especially vital lesson for the spiritually inclined, who, when beginning to find freedom

[12] Hazrat Inayat, Khan, *The Sufi Message of Hazrat Inayat Khan*, Vol. XIII: The Gathas (Geneva: International Sufi Movement, 1982), p, 112.

from conventional visions of reality, can easily think it desirable to leave life's abundance behind. Some who are spiritually oriented tend to be wary of accepting the responsibility and burden of the material world, recognizing that life is indeed impermanent, and concluding that there is little purpose in concentrating too much on what takes place here. But the end result of this is that the care for the material world is given over to those who have less concern for deeper wisdom and values. In this spirit, the poet Rumi offered passionate advice to the seeker:

> *Oh prisoners of water and clay, occupy yourselves with your tasks and acquire skills! Be not brokenhearted! Fear not that your skills remain hidden! For We have placed these pearls and fruits in your treasuries, and you yourself had no knowledge of them. They were concealed in Our Unseen Knowledge. Before entering into existence the skills and beauties that you see today in yourselves were pearls in the Unseen Ocean, hurrying to enter the treasuries of the inhabitants of dry land. We have placed a special characteristic in every possessor of a skill, in every craftsworker and master of a task, whether goldsmith, jeweler, magician, alchemist; and in every tradesworker, lawyer and scholar, so that they will always be bubbling over and displaying their own skill.* [13]

True awakening brings responsibility, and asks of us the blossoming and fruitfulness of our being. Service to life, in turn, leads to true freedom. Affirming our deepest desires, allowing our minds and hearts to become fertile fields, we can give a direction to our lives that helps others and contributes to the world around us.

[13] Jelaluddin Rumi, in William Chittick, *The Sufi Path of Love: The Spiritual Teachings of Rumi,* (Albany: SUNY Press, 1983), p. 200.

3
GUIDANCE AWAITS US

Make peace with the universe.
Take joy in it.
It will turn to gold.
Resurrection will be now.
Every moment, a new beauty.
And never any boredom! [14]

THIS "ALL-POSSIBLE UNIVERSE" is teeming with mystery. Recognizing this depends on our capacity to open to and value what is most simple and most miraculous. Sufi philosophy adds a challenging truth, that Reality—including the reality of the Divine—appears to us in accord with our belief.[15] In other words, if we believe in Mystery, this Mystery will be before us. If we think life consists only in selfish pursuit, we will find ourselves in a pale and flattened-out world.

Quan Yin, Boddhisattva of Compassion, who has vowed to work within this life until all beings are freed from suffering

If we want the widest viewpoint with which to experience a universe of limitless possibilities, we must meet life with awe, stripped of our comfortable theories about the way things are. We can look to both great scientific and spiritual explorers as examples of this practice. The greatest explorers in every realm of inquiry have trusted deeply in the value of questioning their own beliefs. They are very willing to release their fixed concepts, allowing their minds and hearts to open to fresh, naked perception.

Albert Einstein had a great reverence for mystery, and for the

---

[14] Jelaluddin Rumi, *The Book of Love: Poems of Ecstasy and Longing*, trans. Coleman Barks (New York: Harper Collins 2005), p. 110.

[15] This is a central theme of Henry Corbin's *Alone with the Alone: Creative Imagination in the Sufism of Ibn Arabi* (Princeton: Bollingen Series XCI, Mythos edition, 1997). See pp. 124-25 for the discussion of the role of human being in giving form to the "God created in the faiths."

way openness to unknowing allowed him to see things differently. Einstein believed that mystery and unknowing were the sources of all great art and scientific endeavor.

A similar honoring of mystery is found in the account of the last moments of the life of James Clark Maxwell. Maxwell was best known for the elegant equations by which he expressed the connection between light, electricity and magnetism. These equations were crucial for the discoveries of radio waves, x-rays, television and microwaves. About his insights, Maxwell confessed on his deathbed "What is done by what is called myself is, I feel, done by something greater than myself in me."

Opening to Guidance

Guidance can be painful and perplexing. Because it leads us towards new perspectives, it is invariably challenging to our usual ways of thinking. It broadens our scope and radically alters our understanding. But guidance cannot really be effective if we do not allow it: it requires an ability in us to recognize, trust and then act on something that we cannot fully explain by logic, but that our hearts know to be true.

There is a story about Moses that has relevance to each of us, containing essential themes within the mysterious process by which we are guided to our own depths. This story, found in the "Sura of the Cave" in the Qur'an, was identified by Jung as a model for understanding the role of guidance in our journey towards wholeness.

According to this story, Moses opened to guidance not by a humble plea but by a mistake, a certain boasting that resulted in God scolding him. As he was speaking to a crowd, Moses succumbed to pride, believing, if only for a brief instant, that he was the "wisest of men." Immediately he heard an inner voice reprimanding him, telling him that, in fact, "one of Our servants" still walking on the Earth had far superior knowledge. The voice was referring to Khidr, the legendary "Verdant One" or "Green Man" who, like Elijah and John the Baptist, is said to guide souls to "the waters of life" from the desert of ordinary consciousness.

Moses immediately realized his error and asked how to find the wise one referred to. He was instructed that, on his journey into the desert, he should take a live fish with him. At the place where "the two seas join" the fish would disappear and the guide would be found.

Accompanied by Joshua, Moses journeyed. Absorbed in the

difficult travel through the desert, he failed to see the juncture of the seas, and did not notice when the fish leaped in the water and made its way to safety. It was only when he became very hungry that Moses thought of the fish, and then Joshua told him of its departure.

Returning to the spot, Moses encountered Khidr. As Moses met Khidr and expressed his desire to be guided, Khidr warned that Moses could not question him. He said that Moses was simply not patient and trusting enough to endure what would follow. Moses, in his enthusiasm, assured Khidr that he would not question anything. Yet as soon as they begin journeying together, the testing of Moses began. Three times Khidr did things that Moses could not understand or tolerate. The guide's actions seemed strange, cold or senseless, and no ordinary ways of thinking could explain them. Yet, as Khidr would later explain, in each instance there was a supra-logic, beyond Moses' comprehension, accounting for Khidr's actions.

There are numerous other stories and rituals related to Khidr found throughout the world. Khidr is prayed to and honored in springtime festivals in many Turkish villages. He has also been linked with Enoch, whose name literally means "the initiated." Like Khidr, Enoch takes the role of the initiator, bringing the seeker to a sacred meeting place.

Connected also with the traditions of Hermes, the initiations by Khidr lead towards the realization that the everyday world is also the sacred world, well symbolized by the "place where two seas join." Khidr serves to bring us home to ourselves, to our inner guide, where seeming irreconcilables join, where the fish of our own soul leaps into the freedom of the ocean of Being. In most practical terms, meeting with Khidr removes any veils that cause us to separate the "two seas" of inner and outer reality. Khidr thus guides our hearts to the alchemical marriage of heaven and earth, in which all of Reality is realized to be a world of soul and spirit, a life that is ever-evolving towards the manifestation of beauty within and without.

Sufi wisdom urges us to literally "put on the shoes of Khidr." While circumstances will be unique for each of us, inner guidance will take us in directions that we too may not understand, at least at first. Ultimately, the guidance will reveal a correspondence between inner and outer realities, and will allow us to see how vitally important each of these realities is in learning how to care for ourselves and our world. Ultimately, connecting with the "Khidr of the soul" brings spiritual energy and true wisdom to the issues and problems of the life around us.

Pir Vilayat explains our opening to guidance in scientific terms: By opening we are allowing the "self-organizing universe" to act upon us, to transform us. This particular capacity of self-organization usually comes with some disturbance to our comfort, our equilibrium. Here we might think of Christ's teaching that we have to "lose our lives in order to find our lives." In the book *Steppenwolf*, Herman Hesse framed this loss of our conventional ways of thinking as the ticket of admission to the "Magic Theater" of Reality. Like Moses, we naturally hesitate and object, afraid that when we lose our reference point there will be nothing left. But the moment we are so willing, the moment we admit our unknowing and ask Mystery for guidance, the ingenious and intimate Khidr of our soul will offer us companionship and wisdom. From this moment a whole new life begins, an awareness that the universe is a unity rooted in love, in which elegant guidance and events literally conspire to prepare, cultivate and bring to fruitfulness the seed of our humanness.

LED BY MYSTERY (*Appendix to Chapter 3*)

While it is quite easy to think about guidance in abstract terms or in the life of the scientist or prophet, it is quite another thing to truly recognize the guidance being offered to us in our everyday life. Though we do not always realize it, every seeking soul continually meets guidance along the spiritual path. It comes from all directions, urging us to listen and witness, to experience life's magical display, to stretch beyond our doubts and disbelief and open to the miracle of our existence.

We will share below a recent experience of meeting with Ogyen Trinley Dorje, the seventeenth Karmapa and head of the Kagyu lineage of Tibetan Buddhism. To preface this, we observe that the Tibetan people have much to teach us about living very naturally and sanely while also maintaining an extraordinary capacity for the "All-possible." To many Tibetans, things that would be seen as miraculous by Western standards are most natural. For example, when a great teacher is born, comes to give a talk or passes away, it is very common for people to see rainbows.

The recurring rebirth of a teacher is historically linked with the Karmapa, who is said to be the first of the tulkus, the teachers who are reborn to continue their teaching over many centuries. The Karmapas leave precise details about their next birth. The letter referring to the birth of the present Karmapa was hidden in an amulet which his predecessor gave to an esteemed student and friend, the Tai Situ Rinpoche. It was years later that the Tai Situ remembered the words he heard upon receiving the amulet. The Sixteenth Karmapa said, "here, you may need this someday". Upon opening the leather case of the amulet, the Tai Situ found a detailed prediction letter with the exact place of birth and names of the parents of the present Karmapa.

When the present Karmapa was born, the villagers in his hometown reported that a conch and cymbals were heard for three days. All the townspeople also witnessed a rainbow encircling the sun. When the young Karmapa walked in the mountains, rocks that he touched would be left with the imprint of his palms. A mantra might appear as his shawl brushed against a rock. Often, just as the young teacher would enter a room to give a talk, a clap of thunder would sound. Numerous cases are recorded in which the Karmapa either foresaw an event, or told of a past event of which he had no outer knowledge.

In 2004 the authors planned a trip to India. Both of us study Tibetan Buddhism with Lama Norhla Rinpoche of Wappinger Falls, New York, who, coincidentally, announced that same year that he was to sponsor the annual festival for world peace held in Bodhgaya, India. Lama Norhla, one among hundreds of possible lamas to sponsor the festival, had not undertaken this task in many years. To our delight we found that we had booked our itinerary to visit the Buddhist pilgrimage site of Bodhgaya for the exact days of the festival.

Subsequently, we attended a fund-raiser and had contributed some Tibetan calligraphy pieces in order to help raise money for the upcoming festival. At the fund-raiser, one of the monks suggested that we read a recent book about the Karmapa, a fascinating account of his escape from Tibet, his past lifetimes and prophesies about the times of his future incarnations.[16]

Having begun in-depth study of Buddhist teachings only a few years earlier, we knew little of the stories of the Karmapa and his importance to the Tibetan people. We learned that all the practitioners from the Kagyu lineage, and many from other lineages as well, feel deeply connected to this being. They pray for an opportunity to be in his presence, and for a single glance from him, both considered immeasurable blessings.

---

[16] The book is *Karmapa: The Sacred Prophecy* by Thomas Pardee, Susan Skolnick and Eric Swanson (Wappinger Falls, NY: Kagyu Thubten Choling, 1999).

From our reading, we were moved by the tremendous devotion of the Karmapa to helping others, and his wisdom and great strength. We expressed to each other, sincerely but very casually, that it would be wonderful if we met with him on our trip. Given the seeming improbability of such an occurrence, we did not give this a second thought.

Upon arrival at Bodhgaya, we heard that the Karmapa was present at the festival. He was presiding in the afternoon sessions at the bodhi tree, where Buddha sat for forty nine days before his enlightenment. On the day before we left, we found out that he had been giving talks for the English-speaking and Chinese-speaking students the whole week we had been there. We were able to attend his final talk, and where we were astonished by the great presence and wisdom of this profound being at only nineteen years of age.

Our trip to Bodhgaya was very difficult. We drove on wild roads and encountered a blackout, then rifle fire between a posse of police and teenagers. Our taxi driver stopped his car in the middle of the gunfire, paralyzed by fear, and we had to exhort him to drive on instead of sitting in the center of the fight. During our stay we thought we would freeze each night, not at all prepared for the January cold in that part of India. Finally, leaving Bodhgaya and on our way to the airport at Patna, our car was stopped and surrounded by communist demonstrators who had been halting all transportation in the area.

We arrived at Patna airport after many hours of driving. After waiting many more hours for a delayed plane, an announcement was made that the lowering fog ceiling would prohibit our flight. Weary and disappointed, we were bused to a hotel and resigned to another eighteen hour wait for a flight.

The next day, back at the airport, we were almost alone at check-in. As we were just about to go through security, the police stopped us so that an entourage of bodyguards surrounding the Karmapa could pass by us. Surprised and overjoyed, we called out in one voice "Karmapa!" He smiled and greeted us. While waiting for our plane, we sat with him in a small room for forty five minutes of silent and heartfelt communion. We shared a warm farewell as the Karmapa's plane was called and he departed. To this day we still feel the tremendous blessing and inspiration of this meeting, which could not have been consciously orchestrated by the best trip planning or scheduling.

Some readers may wonder why such a meeting was considered so auspicious to us, and why the connection with teachers is so emphasized in most spiritual traditions. Our own teacher, Pir Vilayat, thought it very important in this age that teachers downplay the "guru trip" and do not present themselves as infallible guides to be followed like Khidr. Instead, Pir Vilayat sought to wean his students and allow them to find true independence.

At the same time, Pir Vilayat explained why contact with a "highly enlightened" teacher is so useful. He spoke of his first encounter with a rishi (a contemplative yogi living in a cave), high up in the Himalayas. After months of searching for a genuine holy being, Pir Vilayat encountered this great soul while wandering in the middle of a snowstorm. The rishi invited Pir Vilayat into his cave for the night, which was spent mostly in silent meditation. At one point, the sage turned to Pir Vilayat and said, "Why have you traveled so far to see your own self?" Pir Vilayat did not have an answer. In later years, he would recount this story and say "now I have an answer for that sage: In order to become who we are we have to see ourself in another who is better able to mirror the depth and sacredness of our being than we are conscious of."

Indeed, a similar recognition took place in our meeting with the Karmapa. Sitting with him sparked something in us, and felt like a homecoming to a part of ourselves that we knew and yet had somehow forgotten. And while consciously we knew we were meeting with a great and ancient guide of souls, what we felt was a naturalness, a simple peace, clarity and bliss, rather than reverence or awe. Many people also report the same sense in the presence of the Dalai Lama. These feelings, and our sense of deep connection with the Karmapa, remain with us to this day.

While the forms in which guidance comes may differ, it is ever streaming towards each human being who opens to receive it. It does not only come through the teachers and guides within formal spiritual traditions. We may be fairly confident that, unbeknownst to us, there are many guides silently at work both all around us and on planes of existence that we cannot perceive. To benefit from these beings, we must simply be willing to be open and receive the love, compassion and wisdom that we are being freely offered.

4
THE NATURAL STATE

What gives us the inclination to seek for happiness is the feeling of having lost something which we have always owned, which belonged to us, which was our own self. The absence of happiness, which a soul has experienced from the day it has come on earth and which has increased every day more and more, makes us forget that our own being is happiness.[17]

T HIS IS AN AGE OF GREAT QUES-
TIONING. Many people today are sophisticated enough to question a conventionally imposed identity and the values that go with it. Many are also wise enough not to

Ogyen Trinley Dorje, the seventeenth Karmapa, with the fourth Jamgon Kongtrul in 1996. Both are revered as reincarnations of lamas who taught in America and Europe from the 1960s to the 1980s and emphasized a natural spirituality, rooted in meditation.

stop at a dismal nihilism, but to truly realize that, as Sartre said, "life begins on the far side of despair."

The "work" of the spiritual path is a radical recovery of our true identity, a reconnection with the mystery of who we are. It is an identity that transcends any historical, cultural or spiritual identity:

I am not of the East, nor the West,
not of the land, nor the sea.
I am not from nature's mine, nor from the circling stars.
I am neither of earth nor water, neither of wind nor fire
I am not of this world nor the next, not of heaven,
nor of purgatory.
My place is the placeless, my trace is the traceless.
It is not the body nor is it the soul,
For I belong to the soul of my love.
If once in this world I should win a moment with You,

---

[17] Hazrat Inayat, Khan, *The Sufi Message of Hazrat Inayat Khan*, Vol. 1: The Way Of Illumination (Geneva: International Sufi Movement, 1960), p. 206.

I will put both worlds under my feet and dance forever in joy.[18]

When we begin to pay attention to inner guidance, we find that it is continually stretching us towards this mystery, allowing us to see how we have fooled ourselves. We have accepted substitutes and compensations for what has been forgotten. Yet to come home to life's guidance, however appealing, is something we strongly resist. It asks a surrender, not to a distant God, a guru or a dogma, but to our heart's knowing, to the natural peace, ease and gentleness at the core of our being. It is the surrender of our doubt, fear and mistrust, all that keeps us from the beauty and joy of our true identity. It is a surrender of the prison walls that we created for ourselves, a protection that served us in the past and is no longer useful. Ultimately it is a surrender of every fixed definition of self, and of our interpretations of what is happening around us. What results is both a freshness in our experience of outer life, and an intimate connection to our boundless depths.

The loss of our natural contact with ourselves sets into motion all kinds of compensatory reactions. We try to fabricate what is missing, and so many of our distorted desires and longing for things in this world come from the sense of lack. The problem is that what we long for is so profound and complete that no substitutes can serve. It is the contact with our Source, hidden in the depths of our being:

> But the most wonderful thing about it is that the soul already knows there is something behind this veil, the veil of perplexity; that there is something to be sought for in the highest spheres of life; that there is some beauty to be seen; that there is Someone to be known who is knowable. This desire, this longing, is not acquired; this desire is a dim knowledge of the soul which it has in itself.[19]

At a deep level we know what it is to feel complete and satisfied, to have our thirst quenched and to feel illumined. We know what it is to dissolve in love, to become the fullness and goodness of life itself. Yet we often find ourselves blocked, confused and very judgmental of our weaknesses and limitations. We repeat the negative reactions that lead to painful experiences, and do not know how to act differently.

In Tibetan Buddhism, it is taught that our confusion comes

---

[18] Jelaluddin Rumi, *The Ruins of the Heart,* trans. Edmund Helminski (Putney, VT: Threshold Books, 1981), p. 22.

[19] Hazrat Inayat Khan, *The Sufi Message of Hazrat Inayat Khan,* Vol. IX: The Unity of Religious Ideals (Geneva: International Sufi Movement, 1960), p. 83.

from three central issues of perception. Firstly, we tend to forget that things are impermanent. We see our friend and we think that he or she is the same as yesterday, and will be the same tomorrow. But this friend has changed, and will continue to change, and only appears the same. Secondly, we believe in our separateness and the independence of phenomena. We think of ourselves as an "I," but really cannot identify what it is within us that is the "I." (In the meditation practices, we will use systematic methods to explore this issue). Finally, we feel separate from the totality of existence. Whatever this "I" is, we tend to see it as separate from nature and from other living beings. Yet science assures us that there is nothing in the universe that is truly independent, and that all of life is literally "co-arising." Everything around us affects us and we affect everything. It is actually this interconnectedness and interdependence within life that is the best mirror of the unity behind life, the true reality that we cannot see.

Tibetan Buddhist teacher Chogyam Rinpoche emphasized that striving—for the sole purpose of maintaining a sense of an "I"—is the great illness of the modern Western world. He described this as a kind of aggression towards ourselves, one that we too often fail to recognize. But how do we begin to step out of this confusion?

Meditation offers us an alternative perspective, a consistent "view" that exists in spite of the everyday confusion that we live within. There is a transparency, a lucidity, a field of potential that is behind the scenes and that, through meditation, we can access and bring into our awareness. Meditation is therefore a "work" that counters our striving, not discounting our intention and concentration, but opening us to a deeper current in our being. Practicing meditation, we are actually practicing *living* from our natural self. Resting from striving, we open to fresh wellsprings of life, inspiration and guidance, coming from our depths.

5

RECEIVING THE MAGICAL PALACE

*One tries to build a person-
ality, but once the soul has
awakened, the personality is
built like a magic palace. It
is built without building.[20]*

U NLESS THE LORD
BUILDS THE HOUSE,
THOSE WHO BUILD
IT LABOR IN VAIN.[21] Within
this sobering and mysterious Psalm verse is a cryptic teaching about the way
to bring our spiritual realization to bear on the life

*The Taj Mahal in Agra, India, built according to the
description of heaven found in the writings of Sufi
mystic Muhyiuddin Ibn Arabi*

around us. The teaching calls us to harmonize and align our "work"
with all that is natural, beautiful and exalting. It calls for radically different ways of "working" than we are used to. Instead of aggressive
movement, this way calls us to first listen and receive, opening to the
present, to "what is." It means embracing the most intense of energies acting upon us, akin to the raw elements of rain, snow, hail and
thunder. In the next breath, it can mean receiving the bounty of life or
a tender loving breeze. In essence we are being invited to a profound
and cosmic alchemy, by which our being is continually transformed,
stretched and molded in most unimaginable and yet elegant ways.

The intensity of this process, along with the promise it holds, is
well described by Rumi in his urging that we surrender all that stands
in the way of our unfolding:

Tear down this house.
A hundred thousand new houses
can be built from the transparent yellow carnelian
buried beneath it,
And the only way to get to that

---

[20] Hazrat Inayat Khan, *The Sufi Message of Hazrat Inayat Khan*, Vol. XI: The Magnetism
of the Soul (Geneva: International Sufi Movement, 1964), p. 118.

[21] Psalms 127 (IV).

is to do the work of demolishing
and then digging under the foundations.
With that value in hand all the new construction
will be done without effort.
And anyway, sooner or later,
the house will fall on its own.
The jewel treasure will be uncovered,
but it won't be yours then.
The buried wealth is your pay
for doing the demolition,
the pick and shovel work.
If you wait and just let it happen,
You will bite your hand and say
"I didn't do it as I knew I should have."
This is a rented house. You don't own the deed.[22]

Einstein observed that we cannot solve a problem using the very same consciousness that created the problem in the first place. "Reality itself," says Hazrat Inayat Khan, "has become confused." Somehow we have to step outside of the confusion to attain the fullness of our potential. Our soul, vast and blissful, complete and in need of nothing, has identified itself with our limitation and lack, the smaller domain of our ordinary life. However much we strive, no material or spiritual acquisitions, no efforts at self-improvement are going to bring us out of this predicament. What is needed is the simple and yet radical openness to the cultivating action of the universe upon us.

As we realize and trust the natural process within life to guide and bring forth our essential richness, this openness will increase. At the same time, openness to the action of the universe does not mean being passive. When some new blossoms of awakening finally emerge in our being, there will be a time when our application of will and intention will be crucial. Yet the *first* stages of this process ask us to work in the opposite direction, cultivating receptivity and learning to "allow," from moment to moment, the transforming action of the universe upon us. This is truly a form of meditation in life, which we will explore more fully in the final section of this book.

By concentration and other practices, both within meditation

[22] Jelaluddin Rumi, from *The Essential Rumi*, trans. Coleman Barks. (San Francisco: Harper Collins, 1995), pp. 113-14.

and in everyday life, we learn to receive the priceless gifts offered us. In meditation, openness means watching and not reacting, becoming more comfortable with the disturbing thoughts and emotions that arise and allowing them to fade away of their own accord. Eventually, through this practice of allowing ourselves to rest with deeper thinking and feelings, we become more able to apply the same attitude to the rest of our life. By this we find that our meditations and our lives are simply mirrors of each other, and we are able to meet our life with the same peace and openness that we have within meditation. The ultimate result is that we realize every moment to be complete and to be bearing a gift, be it abstract or concrete, guiding us towards the depths of satisfaction, peace and illumination.

As we noted above, intensity is only one aspect of life we are called to receive. Another aspect is much more subtle, and sometimes requires more skill and intelligence. Turkish Sufi teacher Muzaffer Effendi told a story[23] that highlights the importance of this receptivity and how difficult it can be for us.

Many years ago, in Turkey, a traveler came to a small town. The custom at those times was to open your door to whoever came as "God's guests," as they were called. When someone knocked on your door and said, "I am God's guest," you were to invite him in, feed him and give him a place to sleep.

The traveler came upon a group of townspeople and asked "Is there a kind person in town who has space to put me up for the night? The next morning I will continue my journey." The townspeople said, "Well, yes, there is one person who does welcome guests. If you stay there, he will feed you, put you up and be very kind to you. However, we have to warn you that he has a strange habit — in the morning, when you are leaving, he will beat you up."

It was winter and very cold. The traveler said, "I'm not going to spend the night on the street, hungry. I will go, and I'll take what comes to me. I will at least sleep in a warm room, and if he'll beat me up, he'll beat me up."

The traveler knocked on the door and a very pleasant man opened the door. The traveler said, "I am God's guest." The man replied, "Oh, come in, please come in." He offered the traveler the best place and his best cushions. The traveler replied, "Eyvallah." ("Eyvallah" means "As

[23] The story is from *Love Is the Wine* by Sheikh Muzaffer, ed. by Robert Frager (Los Angeles: Philosophical Research Society, 1987), pp. 81-83.

you wish." It literally means "As God wills" and *signifies our willingness to accept whatever we are given — good or bad, delightful or unappetizing — remembering it comes from God).*

"May I put a pillow behind you to make you more comfortable?" "Eyvallah." "Are you hungry?" "Eyvallah." The host brought a delicious dinner, and then asked the guest if he would like some more. "Eyvallah." The host said, "Coffee?" "Eyvallah." Would you like a cigarette? "Eyvallah." "May I make up your bed?" "Eyvallah." The host made up a wonderfully soft bed and put a feather comforter on it. "Would you like some water before you go to sleep?" "Eyvallah." In the morning the host was up early. He asked the traveler, "Would you like some breakfast?" "Eyvallah." The host served a wonderful breakfast.

Once breakfast was finished the traveler realized it was time to take leave of the host. After the stories he had heard, he was afraid of what might happen, though this man had just devoted almost a day to taking care of him. "I would like to take my leave now," he said, fearfully. The host replied kindly, "Eyvallah," and added "You seem to be a man without much money. Would you permit me to give you some money?" "Eyvallah."

The host gave him ten pieces of gold. The traveler thought to himself, "What a beating I am going to get after this!" The host saw him to the door, saying, "May God go with you. Goodbye."

The astonished traveler said, "I beg your pardon? There is terrible gossip going around about you. You are most generous person I have ever seen. They say that you are hospitable with guests but that in the morning you beat them up. May I go spread the word you do no such thing, that you are a wonderful man and a wonderful host?" The host said, "No, no, what they say is true."

The guest said, "But you did not treat me that way."

"No, you are different. My other guests are much more trouble. When I offer them the best place in the house they say, 'Oh no, no thank you, you sit there.' When I offer them coffee they reply, 'Well, I don't know. I don't want to bother you.' I ask them to have dinner and they say 'No, it will make too much fuss.' Those people I certainly beat in the morning."

We are the guests, beloved by the divine host, and by some irony quite incapable of receiving the gifts that we are being offered. We don't quite know how to receive, to feel worthy of receiving. Wisdom teachings urge us to realize that we are truly this beloved of the Divine, sought by love and called to receive. This requires of us a radical openness, a trust and intimacy that must be honored and affirmed in our being. For this natural receptivity has been covered by our hesitation, our doubt and fear, and our outworn images of a punishing and constraining universe. It may be that by such images we miss many gifts and bring on our own sense of being unloved.

In truth, the "host" wants us to accept a bountiful table spread and is not happy when we don't. The host wishes to offer us the fullness of life, to transform our consciousness, to *create* the magical palace of our being, which from our perspective is "built without building." Instead of emerging through our efforts, this comes by our willingness to receive, to allow ourselves to be fed and fashioned, and to be filled with life energy, intelligence and love.

It is through meditation and spiritual practice that we learn to open to what is being offered us. Suspending our knee-jerk reactions to things, reprogramming ancient ways of defending ourselves from vulnerability, we can root out the confusion, fear and layers of mistaken identity that do not serve us. It is this openness that makes us a fertile field, in which the seeds of new life are planted. In this way, we share in the self-organizing and self-renewing forces of a universe that is always wishing to offer us Her gifts.

6
OUR TRUE BEING IS HAPPINESS

*The soul's very being is happiness.
Once a person is able to clear the
undesirable impressions, a new
power begins to spring, opening a
way to accomplish all one wishes,
attracting all one requires, clearing one's path of all obstacles, and
making one's atmosphere clear—
to live and move and to accomplish
all one wishes to accomplish.*[24]

MOMENTS OF ECSTASY in life remind us of our most natural condi-

*Street children of Delhi, India, who are students
of the Hope Project, started by Pir Vilayat Khan
(see inside cover of this book)*

tion of freedom and happiness. Ecstasy literally means "out of stasis,"
free from anything fixed or stagnant. Freedom and happiness, realized
as the freshness of our true being, naturally overflow into generosity,
love and gratitude.

Ultimately, through the spiritual journey, we gain the capacity
to be joyous even in the midst of suffering. We learn not get completely
caught by circumstances—the traffic jam, the noise, the doctor's diag-
nosis of an illness. No matter what appears, we know another view
that is open and spacious, and that allows us to find an equanimity and
peace with our experience, accepting and even appreciating the most
difficult of feelings and situations.

We seem to be continually distracted and challenged to maintain our happiness. Yet instead of rejecting this challenge, we can recognize that our struggle is a vital force for our unfolding. In this regard, Chogyam Trungpa observed that we are "never so truthful as
when we are cornered." The pressure that limitation places on our vast
souls helps us to go beyond our excessive self-concern. With enough
pressure, we find our consciousness spills over. From a state of pain we
can feel a sudden shift, realizing that we can bear what is happening.
Abiding until our joy returns, we feel ourselves again connected with

[24] Hazrat Inayat Khan, *The Sufi Message of Hazrat Inayat Khan,* Vol. XIII: The Gathas.
(Geneva: International Sufi Movement, 1982), p. 222.

life, vast, flowing and, often to our great surprise, ecstatic.

The struggles of our life exist not because God likes to test us but because the intelligence and beauty of the universe seek to unfold. Something is ever trying to be born within us. The deepest spark in our being wants to burst forth, to bring us to fruition and contentment. For this reason we have to give up our loyalty to fears and doubts, to hesitation and self-defeating habits of mind. We have to be very vigilant in order to avoid sacrificing our ecstasy for the empty and momentary satisfaction of anger, resentment or self-pity. In the language of Pir Vilayat, we come to learn to continually "unmask the hoax" behind such reactions, identifying with a far nobler sense of self. At the same time, we cannot "unmask" disturbing situations simply by an act of will. We have to truly see beyond our dilemmas, but without judgment or rejection of these. Meditation helps us here, making us aware of the fact that life is a malleable substance, and that our bodies, minds and even personalities are as clay that can be shaped.

The practice of meditation is not undertaken to better ourselves or to add something new to our psyches. Instead it is work of self-discovery, a polishing of the mirror of our heart. Ultimately, it will allow us to see tremendous possibilities and spaciousness within the most limiting circumstances we face. If we are willing to serve, we will be given a clear vision of how life is using every circumstance to creatively transform us, to make us fruitful. By not shutting down in the face of difficulty, we not only escape from confusion but gain tremendous freedom, and come into deep and intimate conversation with all of existence.

7

Every Movement Is a Movement of Love

Knowledge without love is lifeless.[25]

T HE THOUGHT THAT AN INTEL-
LIGENT UNIVERSE IS ASKING
US TO AWAKEN is very challenging. Guidance will not lead
us only towards an exalted and
pristine state of consciousness:
instead, we are asked to deeply
embrace the entire spectrum of
human feelings and emotions,
many of which the "spiritually
minded" tend to avoid.

Sufi teachers have been
known to warn over-ambitious
spiritual seekers that they need
not spend too much time in soli-

A Hawaiian dancer

tary meditation, and that, upon physical death, they will have all eternity to meditate. With the exception of a daily practice and an occasion-
al retreat, time is afforded us *to live*, to play some unique note within
the symphony of life. Within our brief and precious moments of earthly
existence, we have the opportunity to immerse ourselves in the bounty
of life, and to live in a state of discovery and gratitude.

Stories from around the world describe how the whole of creation was brought into being as an act of love. From a silent depth,
where all existed as a singularity or unity, there came a sigh, a breath
of love. In one Sufi version, it is said that Divine Passion sought relief
from the solitude of unity, and that even today, in the moments when
our creativity and self-expression are lacking, we re-experience the
same anguishing desire to give birth.

To see love and beauty, we must *become* love and beauty. This
demands of us a sacrifice, and it brings us to feel a great deal of pain.
We have to live most fully in our bodies of clay, within the limitations
and struggles of life, to truly feel and experience the exquisiteness of

[25] Hazrat Inayat Khan, *The Sufi Message of Hazrat Inayat Khan,* Vol. IX: The Unity of
Religious Ideals, (Geneva: International Sufi Movement, 1963), p. 217.

being. In the words of Hazrat Inayat Khan, "Hail to my exile from the Garden of Eden to the earth! If I had not fallen, I should not have had the opportunity of probing the depths of life."[26]

Inayat Khan recounts the story of the angels, who, fearing the earthly journey, refused to enter vessels of clay and become human beings. The Divine played exquisitely beautiful music, enticing the angels to a state of ecstasy. Intoxicated, the angels danced into their bodies.

We are these angels, and we may still carry something of the resistance and fear of fully embracing life on this Earth. So it still remains that our challenge is to fully enter into life, to surrender to its rhythms and seasons, its gifts and its sometimes unreasonable demands. For in the middle of life's struggle we have the possibility of again finding the original intoxicating music, the sacred impulse of love that brought us here.

The Sufi philosopher Muhyiuddin Ibn Arabi describes "the movement of the world from non-existence into existence"—the desire that sparked creation—as Divine Love seeking expression. He heard, in a dream, the Divine speaking through the voice of a prophet: "*I was a Hidden Treasure. I loved to be known and I created the world.*"[27]

Recognizing that every movement in the universe is a "movement of love" is the key to literally decoding the mystery and confusion of life. It is our embrace of the full spectrum of life's constriction and expansion, all that is joyful and all that is painful. The realization is tremendously challenging, and yet it will fill our lives with awe and beauty.

---

[26] Hazrat Inayat Khan, *Complete Sayings* (New Lebanon, NY: Sufi Order Publications, 1978), p. 53.

[27] Muhyiuddun Ibn Arabi, in *The Wisdom of the Prophets*, trans. Titus Burckhardt, (Glouchestershire, England: Beshara Publications), p. 104.

8

THE MONASTERY OF THE WORLD

Renounce the good of the world.
Renounce the good of heaven.
Renounce your highest ideal.
Then renounce your renunciation. [28]

IKOS KAZANTZAKIS, author of *Zorba the Greek*, tells a story of how he was guided to a spirituality that embraced all of life. In his twenties, seeing through the violence and sham of the world around him, Kazantzakis wished to devote himself to spiritual exploration. Wanting the life of a hermit, he decided he would go to live on Mount Athos, the island

Every day up to 10,000 people are freely provided meals prepared by a communal effort at the Golden Temple, Amritsar, India.

of Orthodox monasteries and hermitages off the northern coast of Greece.

Upon his arrival on the island, Kazantzakis was led to a *staretz*, a wise and ancient recluse, who looked deeply into his being. With brief reflection, the teacher said, "Return to your life and discover the monastery of the world." He told the young pilgrim that "the age of the solitary is over," and that a new way of spirituality must be realized.

Kazantzakis was at first very disappointed, but he followed the teacher's guidance. Eventually he married, authored over twenty literary works and became the Minister of Education of Greece. He was also a most powerful voice of resistance against fascism in his country. Kazantzakis lived a full and passionate life—so well reflected in his character *Zorba*.

The guidance that Kazantzakis received, to "discover the monastery of the world," is for each of us. It calls us to first remove any deeply held beliefs or sentiments that cause us to separate spiritual and material worlds. In the language of the Buddhist tradition, the seemingly unsatisfactory world of samsara and the exalted world of nirvana are not separate, but in fact one and the same.

---

[28] Fariduddin Attar, quoted in Pir Vilayat Khan, *In Search of the Hidden Treasure* (New York: Jeremy Tarcher, 2003), p. 67.

The same lesson comes also from the legendary trickster Nasrudin, whom we find sitting in a church with his feet upon the altar. His friend the local priest comes in, shouting, "Nasrudin, never put your feet on something sacred!" Perplexed, Nasrudin looks around: "Oh, forgive me! But where," he sincerely pleaded, "can I put them that *isn't* sacred?"

Meditators who develop a distaste for ordinary life eventually find that their spiritual practices also leave them unsatisfied. Because inner and outer life are intricately connected, one cannot attain the fullness of spiritual realization without the embrace of the precious life of the senses that we have been given. The approaches to spirituality which do not honor the senses bring a tremendous imbalance and one-sidedness, and ultimately work against attainment of peace and harmony in our being.

One case of this downplaying of the senses is the practice of celibacy, often rooted in the belief that the pleasure and intimacy of sexuality are unnecessary and even dangerous to the spiritually inclined. The Sufi teacher and poet Rumi strongly countered this view, explaining that the intimate relationship between human lovers can bring about a transformation that is far more powerful than that gained by a celibate in a monastery. A partnership with deep intimacy demands our fullest humanity, vulnerability and transparency. It brings a purification of our being that is more intense and complete than anything attained by the celibate. Its fruit is described by Ibn Arabi, who saw that through the act of lovemaking one could have the most complete earthly experience of intimacy with "one's Lord." The same realization is found within the tantric tradition of Tibetan Buddhism.

Preceding all of these teachings, Buddha emphasized the importance of a "middle way" of spirituality, in between asceticism and indulgence. It was said that Buddha's full enlightenment came not when he fasted but when, after a long and arduous retreat, he broke his fast with a glass of milk. And while the stubborn ascetic might argue that this seems like an easy way out of spiritual discipline, Rumi observed that it is actually more difficult to embrace all of life's pains and joys with moderation than it is to fast and stand aloof from the world. In truth, maintaining a compassionate, peaceful and inspired condition in the "monastery of the world" is a far greater challenge than doing so in a cloistered and protected environment.

Viewed properly, all of the energies and materials of life are gifts, and they are all profoundly valuable when we are oriented to-wards service to all beings and all of life. It is this service that gives our life meaning and takes us away from irrelevant concerns. In the words of the great mystic Rabi'a,

> O God, if I worship Thee in fear of Hell, burn me in Hell;
> and if I worship thee in hope of paradise,
> exclude me from paradise.
> But if I worship thee for Thine own sake
> withhold not Thine everlasting beauty. [29]

Removing our distinctions between earth and heaven opens consciousness in a most unique way. It allows us to see most clearly that the whole universe is seeking to express its richness and beauty through us. We are here to embrace the human journey and to find within it the deeper currents of being. A great power comes alive by this discovery and by our offering of its fruits to the life around us. There is nothing in the world more important for us to do! In the words of Kazantzakis:

> Everything you do reverberates through a thousand destinies. As you walk, you cut open and create the riverbed into which the stream of your descendants shall enter and flow. When you shake with fear, your terror branches out into innumerable generations, and you degrade innumerable souls before and behind you. When you rise to a valorous deed, all of your race rises with you and turns valorous.

> We are one. From the blind worm in the depths of the ocean to the endless arena of the Galaxy, only one person struggles and is imperiled: You. And within your small and earthen breast only one thing struggles and is imperiled: the Universe. [30]

[29] A.J. Arberry, *Sufism: An Account of the Mystics of Islam* (London: Unwin, 1979), p. 42.

[30] Nikos Kazantzakis, *The Saviors of God*, trans. Kimon Friar (New York: Simon and Schuster, 1960), pp. 72, 105.

9
THE BELOVED INVITES US ALL

The Sufi's God is not in Heaven alone, but everywhere... both within and without. Therefore there is no name which is not the Name of God, and there is no form which is not the form of God, to the eyes of the Sufi. [31]

Sunrise on the Ganges River, Varanasi, India

AN OBSERVATION OF C.G. JUNG remains completely accurate today: the modern human being is in a predicament, lost in this world, desperately "in search of a soul." There is a tremendous need in us to experience the Divine and understand the mystery of our existence, but we do not always know where and how to begin. We might think that only those who have a certain ardor, or a naiveté and "blessed simplicity," can relate to any such search. We also see many seemingly religious or spiritual people acting hypocritically or with violence, apparently far from any deep and authentic experience of wisdom or compassion. Our images and concepts of the "otherness of God" complicate the matter even further, particularly because a sense of intimacy and unity is paramount to approaching our natural condition and spiritual essence.

The dream of our life takes place within a greater Universal dream, literally a palace of mirrors. The Mysterious Beloved behind our life is actually seeking for us, wishing us to know ourselves as Her beloved. However unfathomable it is to our understanding, the Essence of all conspires to be our fulfillment, and thereby *finds Her own fulfillment through our experience.*

We gradually develop a capacity to realize the Unseen as a Beloved, and to know with certainty that our life is ever filled with guidance. We learn, aided by the insight afforded via meditation, to recognize that all of our life can be "read" as a sacred scripture, and that events, signs and symbols all around us call us to greater intimacy.

This Unseen Mystery, which can never be reduced to our projections and idealizations, might best be described as vast and

---

[31] Hazrat Inayat Khan, unpublished talk, "The Sufi's Conception of God."

boundless Love. It is the profoundly deep feeling that Chogyam Trungpa called the "basic goodness" of life. Touching this feeling causes us to yearn, to seek for more of the fullness of the Beloved. We experience ourself as a drop of water seeking the great Ocean, or the moth seeking the flame. Our yearning is also a mirror, the Ocean's longing for us, welcoming our homecoming. The Beloved invites us all:

Dearly beloved!
I have called you so often and you have not heard me.
I have shown myself to you so often and you have not seen me.
I have made myself fragrance so often
and you have not smelled me.
Savorous food, and you have not tasted me.
Why cannot you reach me through the object you touch?
Or breathe me through sweet perfumes?
Why do you not see me? Why do you not hear me?
I am nearer to you than yourself,
than your soul, than your breath.
Who among creatures would treat you as I do?
Dearly Beloved! Let us go toward union
and if we find the road that leads to separation,
we will destroy separation.
Let us go hand in hand,
let us enter the presence of Truth.
Let it be our judge,
and imprint its seal upon our union, Forever.[32]

Every true love relationship is human and divine, painful yet irresistible, overwhelming and transforming. It bewilders and perplexes us, turns us inside out and makes us most aware that our strong sense of separate identity is wholly an illusion.

Coming close to this elusive Beloved becomes our sustenance. Feeling life's inevitable moments of separation from this ocean of Love brings tremendous pain and longing. And yet it is this pain that brings us closer and closer to the depths of intimacy.

The path of the Beloved asks us to dare to love, to love all and to

[32] Muhyiuddin Ibn Arabi, in Henry Corbin, *Alone with the Alone: Creative Imagination in the Sufism of Ibn Arabi* (Princeton: Bollingen Series XCI, Mythos edition, 1997), pp. 174-75.

embrace what is. This proves, time and time again, to be a great challenge, but one that quickly liberates us from our idols, rigid dogmas and subtle evasions of the true gifts we are offered.

As we open most fully to this love, it guides us. Through trust, imagination and a sense of humor, the intricate mystery that stands behind this life, that cares for and nurtures every atom of this existence, becomes perceptible. With conscious and willing intention, continually saying "yes" to the Beloved's invitation, we see how, through every event and circumstance, our hearts are turned and softened, a soil being prepared for the seeds of new life.

PART II: Preparing the Field

Part II describes the preparing of the soil of our being as the clarifying and purifying of the psyche. It describes the inner transformations that take place on the spiritual path, and basic practices for meditation.

Introduction: The Path and Practices of Spiritual Cultivation

This ploughing is ploughed to destroy the weeds of illusion.
—Buddha Shakayamuni

O Wisdom Goddess,
may I cultivate this open field of awareness
throughout my precious lifetime.
O Mother of the universe
shower your grace upon this black and fertile soil!
Be pleased with my intense longing!
Ma! Ma! Ma!
Mundane consciousness is choked with weeds.
How can I till the entire expanse of body and mind?
If I can clear and cultivate even a small section,
my jubilation will know no boundary.
Thorny brambles of negative thoughts and actions
continue to spring from the soil of the heart.
O Warrior Goddess with streaming black hair,
one swing of your sword of wisdom
will cut every egocentric root
and clarify the heart forever.
This useless poet laments:
"My commitment to tilling the ground of my being
is neither consistent nor deep
yet how intensely I long, O Mother,
to taste your most intimate presence,
to merge my soul with the radiance
of your dark blue wisdom feet!"[33]

[33] Lex Hixon, *Mother of the Universe: Visions of the Goddess and Tantric Hymns of Enlightenment* (New York: Quest Books, 1994), p. 57.

B EFORE A FIELD CAN BE PLANTED, a farmer prepares and cultivates the soil, making it soft, moist and fertile. The hard and dry surface of the land must be softened so that tiny seeds may reach air and sunlight. The soil becomes more fertile by plowing, as it is turned over and as a past growth or cover crop decomposes.

In a similar way, the soil of our beings must be prepared for new life. There are parables in many spiritual teachings of gardening or farming, likening the soul to the prepared soil. The central work of the spiritual path is to make our being a prepared soil, in which divine seed may be planted, take root and grow, blossoming and bearing fruit. This requires that we open our being, allowing the soil of our hearts to be turned and exposed to the warm sun of knowledge, and to the purifying rains and winds of the Divine Guidance.

When our mind is like an unplowed field, it is filled with self-defeating scripts and obsessions. When cleared it becomes the living soil of a receptive heart, where guidance is bestowed and new life grows. By opening and entrusting ourselves to the spiritual journey, we are allowing all that might otherwise become hard and brittle to be broken down, turned again and again. Softened and cleared of all that blocks the growth of potent seeds, our true and natural being can effortlessly unfold.

Until we go through this process akin to plowing, we are not so aware of all the places where the soil of our being has become hardened. We hold, often unconsciously, to rigid beliefs, prejudices and grudges, sometimes passed on from generations. Allowing these to soften can be a painful and yet tremendously freeing experience, one that the Sufis have called the "alchemy of happiness."

As we dig deeper, harrowing the soil of our hearts, courage is needed. Every rock and pebble of hardened thought or emotion within our being must be loosened and turned. However difficult, it is this process that brings us to our senses, and to the fullness and bounty of life. In the greater intensity of this process it is most important and valuable most seekers to find an experienced guide.

As scientists are now observing, living systems encountering chaos are able to transform into more resilient and elegant states by completely letting go of their outer structures. By this letting go, these systems realize the greatest scope of possibilities, more "degrees of freedom" by which new and more elegant structures may come forth. In the same way, by meditation, everything in our being must be cleared away, even thoughts and associations that appear to us as good. The ground must be cleared so that there is maximal scope for fresh seeds to take root. Any rigidity, any negative habit, judgment of self or another must be removed by a painful and yet liberating inner surgery.

With all its challenges and difficulties, this work in the field of our being is tremendously freeing. Taking us beyond self-deception, it uncovers a joy that has been buried by life's difficult experiences and burdens. Negative impressions that have accumulated or have simply been reflected on the mirror of soul are cleared.

As anyone who has become free from an addiction knows, new currents of life open whenever a constraining pattern in our being has been softened. The effects of this alchemy reach many others: in the words of the great healer Seraphim of Sarov "Acquire inner peace and thousands around you find salvation."[34] As the life of Seraphim attested, "salvation" is not a distant future state, but a fruitful life here. It is attained by reaching the fertile and potent soil of the heart, where the seeds of the inner life can take root and grow. This is the work that brings us to an Emerald Earth. Let us now begin, with intense commitment, opening to the guidance that is ever streaming towards us.

[34] A. Moore, *St. Seraphim of Sarov: A Spiritual Biography* (Blanco TX: New Sarov Press, 1994), p. 126.

10
THE OPENING OF THE WAY

Sometimes there is a gradual awakening, and sometimes there is a sudden awakening. To some persons it comes in a moment's time—by a blow, by a disappointment, or because their hearts have broken through something that happened suddenly. It seemed cruel, but at the same time the result was a sudden awakening and this awakening brought a blessing beyond praise. The outlook changed, the insight deepened; joy, quiet, independence and freedom were felt, and compassion showed in the attitude. A person who would never forgive, who liked to take revenge, who was easily displeased and cross, a person who would measure and weigh, when his soul is awakened, becomes in one moment a different person.[35]

Doorway to a Shingon Buddhist temple, Mt. Koyasan, Japan

EVERYTHING IN NATURE SEEKS A STABILITY, an equilibrium, as a force of self-preservation. At the same time, without the presence of a destabilizing force, there would be no change, no evolution. The work of Nobel laureate Ilya Prigogine describes clearly how a seemingly disruptive force brings about a subtle and yet profound alchemy. Living systems, when pushed into disequilibrium by turbulent or chaotic situations, "leap" into a more elegant structure when the right conditions are present. Elegance includes a practical dimension; the new structures are better able to meet the demands of the turbulent situation and exhibit greater harmony and beauty.

As in nature, the shocks and intensity of life may, given proper conditions, also bring out greater practicality and beauty in us. Strength,

---

[35] Hazrat Inayat Khan, from a talk given in New York City on January 26, 1926. A version of this talk is found at http://wahiduddin.net/mv2/XIV/XIV_19.htm.

insight, understanding and greater capacities to communicate can come through the unseeming gifts of intensity, struggle and conflict.

Sufi teacher Pir Vilayat emphasized that the evolution of consciousness has more to do with purpose than with cause. When facing a crisis, we can benefit by clearing our conscience, reflecting on those things we might have done to bring about a situation. Yet once we have done this, it becomes more important to recognize that the struggles and tests that come our way are catalysts for our evolution. Often things happen that have nothing to do with past actions, but instead reflect the "pull of the future," deepening and quickening our process of unfolding. These are like the fuel of a refiner's fire, shattering our limiting concepts, making us stronger, often through pain, and helping to bring through our talents and potentialities. The tests invariably make us more alive, free and creative.

Ultimately, then, we come to "read" the situations that stretch and shatter us as pivotal opportunities. We come to recognize that the unseen world of spirit is asking us to stretch, to take continual steps into deeper and deeper levels of unknowing. This is the meaning of spiritual "initiation," the hope and cure for the tremendous isolation that modern people feel:

> *All modern people feel alone in the world of the psyche because they assume there is nothing that they have not made up... that we think we have invented everything psychical — that nothing would be done if we did not do it.... For that is our basic idea and it is an extraordinary assumption.... But through a certain training... something suddenly happens which one has not created, something objective, and then one is no longer alone. That is the object of [certain] initiations, to train people to experience something which is not their intention, something strange, something objective with which they cannot identify.*[36]

Such "initiations" do not suggest that we should all become student of a formal esoteric tradition. When Sufi teacher Hazrat Inayat Khan came to the West in the early 1900s, he found many Europeans and Americans who wished to be so selected as initiates for advanced discipleship. To the disappointment of some of these students, Inayat Khan taught that true initiation was simply an awareness of our bond as human beings, culminating in a willingness to serve the realization

---

[36] Carl Jung, *The Visions Seminars*, in Edward Edinger's *The Creation of Consciousness* (Toronto, Inner City Books, 1984), p. 81.

of all of humanity as one body, beyond distinctions of caste, creed or nationality.

Each human being is offered the opportunity for this kind of initiation, not only once in a lifetime, but time and time again. Outer intensity mirrors something happening within, as the soul is faced with a choice, an opportunity to make a step. Sages tell of being hit on the forehead with a rock, or being offered food from the mouth of an old woman. The recent film *The Matrix* recounted the archetypical pattern of initiation, in which the hero could choose to either fight against the forces destroying life on the planet or refuse and try to ignore what was happening.

Parallel invitations come our way all the time. We sense moments when we face a choice, and may receive something that life is offering us. We are most often being asked to let go of a certain perspective. The more we say yes to such offers, the more they come, and ultimately we find ourselves in a wholly new relationship with life. We are, as Jung's words suggest, being asked to move outside of a self-created dream, and realize a much vaster exploration awaiting us.

Life is continually calling us towards greater awakening, and we do not have to wait for a crisis or a difficult choice in order to receive the sacred food being offered. We have to simply be willing to evolve, to take a courageous step towards something our hearts recognize and understand but our thinking cannot quite grasp. In this willingness, we find that the universe responds. When we listen and attend carefully to the signs all around us, the Emerald Earth begins to reveal Herself in all her meaningfulness and beauty.

11
IN THE DARKNESS BEYOND REASON: KALI'S PLAY

Is unlearning forgetting all that one learns? Not at all. This unlearning means to be able to say with reason, logically, the contrary to what one has learned. It is after this that the realization of truth begins; for then the mind is not fixed any more. And it is then that one becomes alive, for then one's soul has been born. It is then that one will become tolerant, and it is then that one will forgive; for one will understand both one's friend and one's foe.[37]

Temple devoted to the goddess Kali, Varanasi, India

There is great joy in darkness. Deepen it.[38]

OPENING TO A SPIRITUAL PERSPECTIVE is a willing step in the dark. It comes from an admission that we cannot fully fathom what is transpiring in our lives, but know that we are being guided in a deeply meaningful way. As we take this step, *everything* we believed to be true comes under scrutiny, is turned inside out and upside down. With wisdom we give less credence to facts and more to our sense of what brings meaningfulness. We learn to deeply question our judgments, our hasty assessments of right and wrong. We recognize clearly the way that opposites require each other, seeing the joy in sorrow and sorrow in joy.

While our understanding is being challenged and our seemingly stable view of things is being shattered, an awareness emerges that something new is being born within us. In this process we are continually tempted to resist change, to maintain and define our world in ways that we are more familiar with. We may resort to an old habit, create our own crisis, or otherwise attempt to halt the action of the spirit. Yet by remaining open, and by realizing that something is truly being born, we will eventually come to a new horizon. In Rumi's words, "*Something*

---

[37] Hazrat Inayat Khan, *The Sufi Message of Hazrat Inayat Khan.* Vol. VI: The Alchemy of Happiness (Delhi: International Sufi Movement, 1989), p. 274.

[38] Sanai, in *The Hand of Poetry* trans. Coleman Barks (New Lebanon, NY: Omega Publications, 1993), p. 20.

opens our wings. Something makes boredom and hurt disappear. Someone fills the cup in front of us. We taste only sacredness." [39]

In Hindu mythology, the goddess Kali is recognized as the divine energy that stirs up all change in our life. Her action stretches us beyond the boundaries of our present consciousness. She tears us apart, devours us, throws us into infernal regions. Can we have patience and endurance, knowing that pain and disorientation can transform? Can we suspend our judgment, our disappointed expectations, knowing that a painful "little death" ushers in new being, new life? This is what is at stake in inner initiation.

The encounter with Kali has a correspondence to the Eleusinian mysteries of ancient Greece, in which the new initiate was blindfolded, taken underground and asked to traverse unknown terrain. Eventually, the blindfold is removed and the neophyte sees the very same terrain illuminated.

What is happening in this mysterious alchemy is a purification. All the seeming darkness and devouring is a clearing away, a melting of our resistance to the Creative Beauty of our depths. The challenge of awakening is simply an acceptance of the process, a willingness to endure whatever it takes for the dawning of new vision and new life. Sometimes this requires a great deal of faith and imagination, a sense of hope that is not based on any reward or even any expectation of relief from pain.

As we awaken, we realize most fully and clearly that there is a collective madness all around us. The reason change is so intense is that we have all strayed so far from the pure and open space of our natural being. To awaken fully, we have to simply allow all the artificial strictures and habits of thought that veil us from clear perception to dissolve. This is what the opening to our depths is leading us towards.

While we do not go through the formal initiation rites of an ancient world, each being who has somehow said "yes" to spiritual awakening is called to these territories of unknowing, uncharted worlds where there is no safety and no certainty of outcome. By responding to this call we open to feelings of abandonment and of being stretched to our limit. At the same time, in our helplessness, we realize the need for refuge in something outside of ourselves, our families and our social networks. This is a great step forward, a choice to depend on

[39] Jelaluddin Rumi, *The Essential Rumi*, trans. Coleman Barks (San Francisco: Harper Collins, 1995), p. 281.

a greater orchestration of events, both within and without, than our own planning and organizing could bring forth. It is a radical shift for most modern people, who have come to value a very stubborn form of self-reliance. Yet by calling out to the unknown for help, by opening to and surrendering to mystery, we gain freedom from the unreliable crutches of pride and self-importance. This experience, which begins with a sense of abandonment, eventually brings an ease and a direct experience of being embraced and cared for by all of life.

The spiritual journey is amazingly precise in shining light on every self-imposed obstacle in our being, every constraint we place on our soul's freedom. This is the play represented by Kali, who helps us become very familiar with dying and becoming. The journey shows us tendencies and reactions that have been buried—our misguided protections from grief and anger, from loss and betrayal, from feelings of isolation. With patience and compassion, these knots untangle and wellsprings of freshness arise. Mysteriously, we realize that even what has been buried has served most precisely in the course of our life's unfolding:

With all errors and mistakes and lacks which we find in our external life, we see a perfect hand working behind it all. And if we looked at life a little further than we look at it generally, we would certainly find that all the lacks and errors and mistakes and faults sum up into something, making life as complete as the wise hands which are working behind it wish it to be.[40]

12
THE CURE IN THE PAIN

The grief you cry out from
draws you towards union.
Your pure sadness
that wants help
is the secret cup.
Listen to the moan of a dog
for its master.
That whining
is the connection.
There are love dogs
no one knows the names of.
Give your life
to be one of them. [41]

W E ARE TRAVELING SOULS, journeying very briefly through this world. We have a faint recollection of where we came from, an original state of unity. That state was vast and expansive in comparison to the constriction we often feel within physical existence.

Somewhere in our journey from the inner planes to this world, there has been a blanking out: we have forgotten where we came from. Descending into the world of matter, we are indeed like strangers in a strange land. Life is too dense, too coarse for the most refined parts of our being. Yet this alienation has been necessary, giving us a context and a kind of raw material to work with. Somehow, in the fog and chaos of the world rather than in heavenly spheres, we have a great opportunity to realize most profound beauty and richness. Still, most people seem to simply get lost, confused and overwhelmed by life.

There are many tales in the sacred traditions of the wayfarer and of the soul's desire to return home, to reconnect to what is real. We mentioned the film *The Matrix*, one such story, which is loosely based on the Gnostic Hymn of the Pearl.[42]

The Hymn of the Pearl, found in the Gnostic Gospel of Thomas,

[41] Jelaluddin Rumi, *The Essential Rumi.*, transl. by Coleman Barks (San Francisco: Harper Collins, 1995), p. 156.

[42] A version of this tale by G.S. Mead and entitled the *Hymn of the Robe of Glory* is found at http://www.gnosis.org/library/grs-mead/grsm_robeofglory.htm.

tells of a royal child sent to a foreign land, to win a "pearl of great price." In order to fit into the strange world, the child learns to eat the local food, wear the clothes and use the language of the land. Yet in the course of this adaptation, the child forgets its parents, its royal heritage and homeland. Eventually, feeling completely lost, the traveler desperately seeks knowledge of how to journey back to his homeland. The remainder of the story tells how the child meets a spiritual guide and learns the way back home.

The story speaks of our sense of exile, although in truth we have never really lost our connection to our source. In fact, as both quantum physics or Buddha's insight would confirm, in a universe that is an indivisible unity, it is virtually impossible to be truly apart from our source. Still, we often *feel* ourselves to be isolated, caught in an extreme sense of separateness.

The poet Rumi likens our condition to that of a reed that has been cut from a reed bed, and the cure for this painful separation is only found *in the pain*. In his words, "If you wish to be more intimate with the Beloved be intimate with the sadness of your heart." He describes how the reed's crying out, its plaintive tone, becomes the prayer by which it reconnects to its source.

What we may not so easily see is that our separation is a mirror. It is not only our pain, but that of Unseen Mystery, who longs also for a seemingly impossible union with its Beloved—with each of us.

Regardless of which side we look from, the pain of separation is the catalyst for divine intimacy. We are not always sure of the way home, and may not be able to fathom that anything can relieve the pain of our loving heart. But if we do feel this pain, this longing, we are actually much better off than being oblivious to our predicament. In truth, when we are in touch with intensity and longing we are exactly where we are supposed to be. In such a condition, we are able to learn a tremendous amount from every situation, and find freedom and spaciousness in spite of circumstances.

Rumi exhorts us: "*Know your true address, from which you came.*" Knowing this, pain and darkness are merely the substance, the *prima materia* we work with in the profound alchemy of our being. When we accept the pain and intensity that comes to us, what could have been unbearable opens us into new dimensions, and eventually brings us to the fulfillment of our lives.

In the Hymn of the Pearl, the "pearl of great price" is not gained by simply returning home to one's source, as this would make life a somewhat pointless venture. Rather, the fulfillment comes, as Christ taught, by remaining "in the world but not of the world,"—reconnecting with our source while being fully involved in everyday life. By this comes a reconciliation of seeming opposites—the "pearl of great price" being gained by appreciating and making a contribution to the profound beauty of this life.

There is a unique challenge for the spiritually oriented soul in the course of this journey. The poet Hafiz offers a metaphor of life as a sea journey, and our spiritual awakening as an impending arrival at a new port. He speaks of how, before landing, the soul gets frightened, thinking it may be attacked, or somehow will not be able to return home. But Hafiz urges that we not stop before completing this journey. Hazrat Inayat Khan explains:

> *The attitude of Hafiz is to land there. Risk it. If it is an attractive place, he is ready to be won. If it will crush him, he is ready to be crushed. This is the daring attitude. Not running away from the false world, but in this false world to discover glimpses of the true. And in this maze to find God's purpose.*[43]

We need courage to persevere, to live the life we are given, to really win the pearl that we are here to win. Ultimately we are to find that this strange and foreign land is not so alien after all and that we can—amidst pain and limitation—realize the fullness of joy and intimacy.

---

[43] Hazrat Inayat Khan, *The Hand of Poetry*, trans. Coleman Barks (New Lebanon, NY: Omega Publications, 1993), p. 140.

13
VULNERABILITY

There is a brokenness
out of which comes the unbroken,
a shatteredness out of which blooms
the unshatterable.
There is a sorrow
beyond all grief which leads to joy
and a fragility
out of whose depths emerges strength.
There is a hollow space
too vast for words
through which we pass with each loss,
out of whose darkness
we are sanctioned into being.
There is a cry deeper than all sound
whose serrated edges cut the heart
as we break open to the place inside
which is unbreakable and whole,
while learning to sing.[44]

SINCE OUR EARLIEST YEARS, self-protective mechanisms have kept us at arm's length from our true identity and true life. With few exceptions, these protections have long outlived their usefulness. In the spiritual journey, we simply have to leave these behind, again becoming vulnerable and opening to our depths.

The words of Christ hint at our need to again become truly vulnerable: "*Unless you turn and become as little children, you can in no way enter the kingdom of heaven.*"[45] Being like a child means opening, being curious, trusting in the ways that the Universe seeks to teach us. Jung, citing an ancient alchemical text, describes this childlike nature as the key to our wholeness:

I am an orphan, alone; nevertheless, I am found everywhere. I am one,
but opposed to myself. I am youth and old man at one and the same time.
I have neither father nor mother, because I have had to be fetched out of

[44] Rashani, used by permission.

[45] Matthew 18:3.

46

the deep like a fish, or fell like a white stone from heaven. In woods and mountains I roam, but I am hidden in the innermost soul of man. I am mortal for everyone, yet I am not touched by the cycle of eons.[46]

Becoming open as children, pulling away the self-protective veils from our psyches, we find profound mystical vision but also tremendous pain. It is this vulnerability that allows us to meet life with a child-like enthusiasm and humility. The greatest of teachers are first to touch their foreheads to the ground, acknowledging a reliance on a universal power that sustains and heals.

In our vulnerability, in our brokenness, is the tender and sometimes suffering spark of our divinity. Here is a treasure, a diamond that has become hidden. Here, more than anywhere else in our universe, we find how we join with the Divine as our most natural self: vulnerable and yet somehow resilient, often puzzled and lost, sometimes nearly broken and always longing to feel connected.

Our inner vulnerability is not always endearing. It can be very easy for us to reject this "being" or his/her counterpart among the homeless on the streets of a city. But we can discover that what we might readily reject is the cover over a precious gem, over a natural and life-affirming passion that has a divine origin. [47]

Attempting to mask our vulnerability takes a great deal of energy. When the wellsprings of our creativity are blocked, when we take ourselves and the drama of our lives much too seriously, we begin to overcompensate. Our frustration, our sense that something is wrong or missing in our life, comes from feeling distant from our source and from the fertile field of our being.

In touching our essential nature, we are both vulnerable and yet very strong. We can feel the most tender feelings and still be in touch with the primal forces of nature. We can feel true gratitude for life, realizing our utter dependence upon its simplest gifts.

---

[46] C.G. Jung, *Memories, Dreams and Reflections* (New York: Pantheon Books, 1983), p. 227.

[47] Sufi thought recognizes this desire as the impulse of "a Hidden Treasure seeking to be known." We explore this theme more fully in Chapter 23.

14
ON BEING TESTED

Dance, when you're broken open.
Dance, if you've torn the bandage off.
Dance in the middle of the fighting.
Dance in your blood. Dance when
you're perfectly free.[48]

T HERE IS A STORY OF ST. TERESA OF
AVILA riding in a horse-drawn
cart. A wheel falls off the cart,
and Teresa finds herself face down in
the mud. She cries, "Lord, no wonder you do not have many friends, if
this is how you treat them!"

Marpa with his disciple Milarepa

In truth, the journey back to
our natural state is full of struggles.
The further we travel on the spiritual path, the more these struggles
confront us. The lives of Buddha, Jesus and Mary, Joan of Arc, Muhammad and his daughter Fatima, and practitioners from all the spiritual
traditions of the world testify to this.

In the Qur'an it is said that no soul is ever tested beyond its
capacity. And yet it seems that we are sometimes challenged right to
this limit! Perhaps it is literally true that those closest to the sacred are
most tested. Yet we are truly all loved by the Divine, and each of us is
continually being asked to stretch. This painful stretching is not simply
punishment for which we are singled out, or a sign of divine malice.
However difficult, our tests and trials give us a greater capacity, and
help us to become like great fruit-bearing trees. The key is in using
what comes our way as a blacksmith would use a forge, allowing our
experiences to mold us and bring us to a fuller and more creative life.

How we view being tested is crucial. We can choose to take it too
personally, too much to heart, or to see it as uniquely tailored gift, a
highly specific medicine administered for our healing and for the well
being of others. Adopting the latter interpretation—seeing what is taking place as a "remedy" for us and those around us—has a magical and
alchemical quality. In fact, even if at times we feel we are perfectly jus-

[46] *The Essential Rumi*, transl. by Coleman Barks with John Moyne (Princeton, New
Jersey: Castle Books, 1997), p. 281.

tified and accurate in seeing something as a personal insult or injury, realizing instead that we are not a target but a transducer of energy literally brings a liberation. By not reacting, we somehow stop forces of negativity in their tracks, and all involved benefit. The overall effect is a clearing of the clouds of confusion around us.

While our circumstances are always unique, we may learn much from the struggles of spiritual pilgrims of the past, such as the great Buddhist sage Milarepa. Milarepa was a student of Marpa, the latter a most renowned translator of sacred texts. Milarepa was tried continually for many years by his teacher. For example, he was instructed to build a house for Marpa's son. Each time the house neared completion, Marpa told Milarepa that he wasn't satisfied with the work or had "changed his mind" about the design. Again and again Milarepa had to demolish the building and begin anew.

While dealing with brick and mortar, Marpa was actually teaching his student on a symbolic level. Such radical destruction and reconstruction is inevitable on the spiritual journey. And while the training of Milarepa can sound rather cruel, it is said Marpa secretly wept when witnessing the trials that his beloved disciple had to go through. Yet Marpa knew that this testing was necessary, a way of preparing and expediting the fullest awakening of his great disciple, whose life was destined to touch untold numbers of beings. From the tests he endured, Milarepa's compassion, wisdom, patience and endurance ripened. Now just hearing Milarepa's name is a joy and a blessing to Tibetan people.

Parallel examples of such testing are found in the life of the prophet Muhammad. Though surrounded by aggression and violence, Muhammad was always most gentle and loving. Each day on his way to prayers, he would walk by a woman who cursed him and threw garbage on him. He never complained of this woman, nor stopped to return her admonishments. But when the woman did not appear one morning, the Prophet was so concerned about her welfare that he went to her house. Her husband could not believe his eyes when he found Muhammad at the door inquiring about the woman's well-being.

Be it Muhammad or Milarepa, or be it Shiva, who allowed snakes to bite him, the greatest of souls are conduits for the projections of people and even of whole societies, and from their difficult situations bring forth healing power. The basic wisdom of not reacting that was followed by these guides is found in the Dhammapada, a sacred

Buddhist scripture:

> *What we are today comes from the thoughts of yesterday; and our present thoughts build our life of tomorrow....* "*He insulted me, he hurt me, he defeated me, he robbed me.*" *Those who think not such thoughts will be free from hate. For hate is not conquered by hate. Hate is conquered by love. This is the law eternal.*[49]

Spiritual tests coming to us are like a surgeon's probe under bright light. They bring to the surface anything in us that needs to be healed. Yet, at the same time, the "tests" are not always sent to cure some ailment in our being. They may actually have to do with healing others. In other cases, the tests may not have to do with healing at all, but simply be as lightning bolts of energy, sent to unleash creativity and life force in us or in everyday situations.

The thirteenth-century Sufi teacher Abdul Qadir Jilani gives further insight about the tests along the spiritual path. He describes how, in the stages of testing, the Unseen may take everything away from us. This early stage can be very painful, and it may appear that we are simply left abandoned and with nothing. Then, to our surprise, a wholly different test comes: we find ourselves being called to "receive our portion," our destiny. Now the Unseen brings to us our heart's desire, a great fullness and abundance that is often more difficult to accept than the losses we have experienced.

So as not to be too complacent about the advent of this stage, Jilani suggests that it requires us to "become like a polo ball" in order to receive our portion. In other words, we allow ourselves to be knocked about by destiny, and thereby truly play whatever part life asks of us. And while this may sound quite dysfunctional to modern psychology, it is in fact evidence of a very mature stage of spiritual realization. To maintain such a condition one must be deeply creative, spontaneous and in touch with the fullness of being. It represents a true surrender, an act of joyful and loving service. As a free choice and expression of true faith, it acknowledges a guiding intelligence at work in our lives, orchestrating events in ways that are beyond our understanding but that bring us greater life and inspiration.

Perhaps the best response to the bewilderment of this stage of spiritual testing is seen in the Hindu god Shiva. Shiva dances in ecstasy in the middle of constriction and limitation. While surrounded by flames

---

[49] *Dhammapada*, trans. Juan Mascaro (New York: Penguin Books, 1973), p. 35.

of fire, he has one foot on the earth and the other raised, displaying his capacity to dance through any circumstance. He can dance because he knows that he is free and that his captivity is truly non-existent. By the dance, the most difficult situation is transformed, used to benefit all, to bring richness and beauty to an otherwise barren world.

Without a doubt, the trials of the spiritual path do come our way. Yet, as love allows us to courageously meet pain and not retreat in fear, we find an unfailing remedy for a world tearing itself apart, and are able to dedicate ourselves to the great task of healing and awakening.

Through love, ripened grapes are crushed to become fine wine. Every blow to the heart opens us, transforms us and ripens us. The coal turns into a diamond with pressure and heat. We surrender to the threshing as the grain in the millstone to make ourselves into bread.

> *When love beckons to you follow him,*
> *though his ways are hard and steep.*
> *And when his wings enfold you yield to him,*
> *though the sword hidden among his pinions may wound you.*
> *And when he speaks to you believe in him,*
> *though his voice may shatter your dreams*
> *as the north wind lays waste the garden.*
> *For even as love crowns you so shall he crucify you.*
> *Even as he is for your growth so is he for your pruning.*
> *Even as he ascends to your height and caresses*
> *your tenderest branches that quiver in the sun,*
> *so shall he descend to your roots*
> *and shake them in their clinging to the earth.*
> *Like sheaves of corn he gathers you unto himself.*
> *he threshes you to make you naked.*
> *He sifts you to free you from your husks.*
> *He grinds you to whiteness.*
> *He kneads you until you are pliant;*
> *and then he assigns you to his sacred fire,*
> *that you may become sacred bread for God's sacred feast.*
> *All these things shall love do unto you*
> *that you may know the secrets of your heart,*
> *and in that knowledge become a fragment of Life's heart.*[50]

---

[50] Khalil Gibran, *The Prophet* (New York: Knopf, 1923), pp. 5-6.

15
ENTERING THE STREAM

A chickpea leaps
almost over the rim of the pot
where it's being boiled.
"Why are you doing this to me?"
The cook knocks him down
with a ladle.
"Don't you try to jump out.
You think I'm torturing you.
I'm giving you flavor,
so you can mix with spices and rice
and be the lovely vitality
of a human being."[51]

WHEN OUR HEARTS ARE AWAKE, we cannot fail to recognize the guidance that is ever coming our way. Each seeming crisis, each intense experience that we face, yields greater intimacy, pulls us closer to the essence of our being. The grain is brought to the millstone, the grapes are crushed, the coal is subjected to heat, fire and pressure, all to bring out flavor, essence and beauty.

Pir Vilayat likens spiritual vision to a game of three-dimensional chess. At a certain point, our life, as if played on the two-dimensional chessboard, inevitably meets with checkmate. Somehow our forward movement stops, and nothing can fill the void of meaning that opens before us. When this happens, and when confusion overwhelms us or pain goes deep enough, our soul longs for a cure.

If indeed life is akin to the two-dimensional board, there would be no cure: the game must end by an inevitable checkmate. The spiritual path, however, opens us to another direction of movement, akin to building a raised perimeter around the chessboard. New ways of seeing and meeting reality open to us.

In the Buddhist tradition this opening heralds the "entering of the stream" on the spiritual path. We are offered the opportunity of taking refuge from the world of appearances, through a most subtle

---

[51] *The Essential Rumi*, trans. Coleman Barks (San Francisco: Harper Collins, 1995) p. 132-33.

surrender to the greater current running through life.

The metaphor of "entering the stream" is very appropriate. With the dawning of awakened consciousness we feel ourselves being drenched, over and over again, with fresh water. Every pore of our being, every strand of thinking, every interest and intention of our soul must be touched by the water of unknowing, preparing us to enter fully into the powerful current that leads to the great ocean of Being.

Our willingness to enter this stream may indeed begin with the feeling of great constriction, a checkmate, but this is eventually eased by the dawning certainty that profound mystery is knocking at the door of our being. Fully entering the stream of awakening is a leap into the arms of this mystery, allowing a challenge to our picture of reality. It is a leap that demands courage but invariably carries the promise of freshness, spaciousness, freedom and ease. It takes a bit of foolishness and humor on our part, a willingness to sacrifice our serious illusions of self and our seemingly reliable vision of reality. This is a leap that restores lightness, curiosity and playfulness in our lives. It is, at one and the same time, a birth, a death, a play of love and a discovery of the meaning of what Pir Vilayat called "resurrection within life."

Most of all, love teaches us to bear pain. A Sufi hymn urges, *"Strive to become a true human being, one who knows joy, one who knows pain...."* Inayat Khan describes pain as the "dynamite that breaks open the heart." Indeed, pain does break us open, makes us uncomfortable and, ultimately, allows us to turn to our own depths to know true intimacy. And like the heat and pressure that forms the diamond, pain opens us to our own resourcefulness, the precious depths of our natural being that is waiting to blossom and bear fruit.

The love stream is a baptism of fire, not just of water. There is a Chinese aphorism: *"Real gold does not fear the hottest fire."* Here we can look to Moses, drawn by the burning bush, falling into a swoon and thereby encountering the Divine. Similarly, Abraham was put into the fire by the tyrant Nimrod, only to experience the fire as cooling and as a rose garden.

When we confront fire, we are humbled. Fire makes us realize we are beginners in our abilities to bear truth and pain. Here it is most important to know our capacity, to learn how to "be cooked not burnt" by the pain and hardships we encounter in our lives.

A Shaker song captures most beautifully the outcome of this difficult step into the unknown:

'Tis a gift to be simple, 'tis a gift to be free
'Tis a gift to come down where we ought to be
And when we have come down to the place just right
We will be in the valley of love and delight
When true simplicity is gained
To bow and to bend we shan't be ashamed
To turn, turn, will be our delight
'Til by turning and turning we come round right.

All our experiences on the path of awakening are homecomings to our unity with all of Being. Our most intense experiences help us see, day by day, that we are guided and loved, under the watchful eye of a compassionate Mystery, ever appreciative and supportive of our journey.

16
The Heart's Natural Pitch

No one can keep us from car-
rying God wherever we go.
No one can rob His name
from our heart as we try
to scale our fears and despair,
and finally accept Happiness.
We do not have to be jealous
of tales of saints
or glorious intoxicated souls
who can make outrageous love
with the Friend.
Our yearning eyes, our warm,
needing bodies,
can all be drenched
in contentment and Light.
No one anywhere can keep us
from carrying the Beloved
wherever we go.
No one can rob His precious Name
from the rhythm of our hearts, steps and breath. [52]

A musician-healer tuning the heart of a
mother camel in the film, The Story of the
Weeping Camel.

I N THE FILM *THE STORY OF THE WEEPING CAMEL,* a mother camel refuses to care for her firstborn. After the very hard labor, the mother is agitated, ill at ease, and will not nurse her colt. She turns away as the colt approaches, not wanting to be bothered. The herders, a Mongolian family in the Gobi desert, realize that a healing is needed, and call upon a skilled musician and a singer who use their song and music to heal. The musician places his violin at the camel's side, near the heart. The wind plays gently on the strings. Then the violin is removed and the singer begins to sing, stroking the mother camel. The violin is then played, and deep, resonant notes sounded. Other camels gather and watch. First a single tear comes to the camel's eye. After a time, many tears follow. Within a few minutes the young colt is brought to the mother, who welcomes her with affectionate nudges as she never had

[52] Hafiz, *The Subject Tonight Is Love,* trans. Daniel Ladinski (North Myrtle Beach, NC: Pumpkin House Press, 1996), p. 53.

before, and then freely allows her to suckle.

Wise native healers understand that every organ of the body has a natural pitch. When our heart has lost its pitch, when it is disturbed by a painful experience or the jarring effect of life's stresses, our entire physical, mental and spiritual well-being is also disturbed. Sometimes even the slightest perturbation of the heart can make the difference between a sense of well-being and feelings of being out of synch with life. Conversely, when an instrument is properly tuned, striking a single note brings great magnetism and resonance. If an instrument can have that magnetism, how much greater is the magnetism of a living heart that is tuned to a deep level of love and harmony! In tune, we are naturally ecstatic, joyful and in touch, bringing pleasure to ourselves and others.

The mother colt had lost her natural sense, her innate instinct, perhaps through the pain of the difficult birth of her colt. This is exactly what happens to us. The impressions of life's struggles and blows must be somehow released so that the heart can return to its natural pitch.

Hazrat Inayat Khan, a master musician, described spirituality in the language of music. He taught that spirituality is simply the tuning of the heart to its natural pitch and, from this harmony, tuning our whole being to the music that resonates through all of life. As the meeting place of inner and outer realities, the tuned heart can harmonize with all the conditions of life and all the inner challenges we face.

Tuning means changing a vibratory frequency. "Being in tune" is part of modern language, and we intuitively understand its meaning. We know from physical exercise that the "tuning" of our body allows our whole being to benefit, as a result of the free circulation of blood and the rhythmic flow of air in and out of the lungs. The same result comes through deep concentration, when mental and psychic stresses are relaxed and a natural sense of harmony and peace is attained.

The tuned heart feels pain acutely, but does not hold on to this pain. Meeting life with the openheartedness of the child, the heart in tune can feel intense sadness and pain in one moment and, in the next, be lifted on a current of joy.

The tuning of the heart is a science and an art, almost lost to the seemingly sophisticated modern world. Its effect is contagious, and by regaining the art of tuning ourselves we are helping to tune the hearts of others around us as well.

For this tuning to be complete, anything disturbing that we are holding onto must be released. The added challenge and complication is that we cannot simply use our will and bring this release. At first all we can really do is to make an intention to let go, to release the past, release ourselves and others from any confusion that caused harm.

When this spiritual journey begins and the heart begins to open, buried feelings do arise. Sometimes thorns of irritation and anger, covering deeper feelings of insecurity, unworthiness and disconnection, come to the surface. As this happens, we come to realize that a similar music to that which healed the mother camel is available to us. Our life, and our letting go, will provide this music. Each impression that is released, forgiven, accepted or simply understood loosens the tension in our hearts and restores us to our natural pitch. Each veil removed brings us more deeply into the heart of Being.

Pir Vilayat often told a story about forgiveness. For years, in his seminars in the United States and Europe, he stressed the value of forgiveness, not only for our own unfolding but for the betterment of the world. Once a lady approached him and said that the teacher only made her feel worse about herself, as there were people she really could not bring herself to forgive.

In reflecting on the woman's words, Pir Vilayat realized that he too was still holding a deeply buried resentment. His sister, Noor-un-nisa Inayat Khan, a British intelligence agent during World War II who worked for the French Resistance, had been tortured and executed by the Nazis in a concentration camp. Pir Vilayat had come to know the identity of the woman who had betrayed his sister for money. A few nights after his encounter with the lady from his seminar, he was awakened to a presence in his room. It was a vision of Christ, who acknowledged that he knew Pir Vilayat could not feel any forgiveness for the woman who had betrayed his sister. But could he, Christ asked, forgive for the sake of humanity's healing, for the sake of all? To this request Pir Vilayat could honestly say, "Yes."

The cure of our strife, our burden, is found in the softening and tuning of our hearts. The beautiful pearls of our own humanity are found by embracing and forgiving the pain caused to us, and by recognizing and asking forgiveness for the pain and confusion that we have caused. This will bring us to our natural pitch and happiness, and brings harmony and healing to the life around us.

17
WORKING WITH IMPRESSIONS

The Chinese and the Greeks
were arguing as to who
were the better artists.
The king said, "We'll settle this
matter with a debate."
The Chinese began talking but the
Greeks wouldn't say anything.
They left.
The Chinese suggested then that
they each be given a room to work
with their artistry,
two rooms facing each other and
divided by a curtain.

The Chinese asked the king for a hundred colors,
all the variations, and each morning they came
to where the dyes were kept and took them all.
The Greeks took no colors. "They're not part of our work."
They went to their room and began cleaning and polishing the walls.
All day every day they made those walls
as pure and clear as an open sky.
The Chinese finished and they were so happy.
They beat their drums in the joy of completion.
The King entered the room
astonished by the gorgeous color and detail.
The Greeks then pulled the curtain dividing the rooms.
The Chinese figures and images
shimmeringly reflected on the clear Greek walls.
They lived there, even more beautifully,
and always changing in the light.
The Greek art is the Sufi way.
They don't study books of philosophical thought.
They make their loving clearer and clearer. No wantings, no anger.
In that purity they receive and reflect the images of every moment,
From here, from the stars, from the void.
They take them in as though they were seeing
with the lighted clarity that sees them.[53]

[53] Rumi, *The Essential Rumi*, Coleman Barks, trans. (San Francisco: Harper Collins, 1995), pp. 132-33.

Rumi's story of the Chinese and Greek artists is obviously not a stereotyping or critique of cultural differences in artistic methods. It is, rather, a symbolic teaching on the value of polishing the mirror of the heart.

After plowing, the traditional farmer harrowed the field with a long-toothed rake in order to further prepare the soil, removing smaller but potentially damaging obstacles to the growth of seeds and plants. Small roots and stubble, rocks and pebbles were cleared. For spiritual growth, a parallel process takes place in our being, obstacles clearing away through the purifying forces of concentration, meditation and openness to inner guidance. This challenging work—the polishing of the mirror of the heart—is the sacred artistry that Rumi alludes to above and that unveils profound beauty.

It is easy for us to understand, in theory, the idea of preparing and laying bare a field for planting. When it comes to our own souls, it can sometimes be difficult to see why we have to allow such a complete and sometimes painful purging of our minds and hearts. Yet transformation of our being is not possible without a clear field, without the removal of any hardened reference points by which we have defined ourselves. Even seemingly desirable characteristics that we identify with must be allowed to dissolve in order to find true freedom and the living, creative spark of our natural being.

Hazrat Inayat Khan likens our being to a silken cord that has been tied in knots. The knots—all the impressions, beliefs, attitudes and emotional filters that have accumulated in the course of our lives—have been drawn tight. These bind our hearts, constricting us and asserting themselves most unexpectedly and undesirably. Wherever such a knot exists, we are robbed of our creativity and happiness. When we unravel these knots—especially the scars of our pasts and anxieties about our future—we feel a great freedom and our thoughts no longer hold a heavy sway over us.

Another image used by Hazrat Inayat Khan to understand the play of the mind is the old-fashioned phonograph record. The impressions we hold are lines in our minds, like the grooves in the record. The same tune plays over and over again, unless we somehow make these lines smooth. Meditation is the key to this process.

Anyone who has struggled with a habit, such as addiction to tobacco, knows all about the presence of strong and recurring lines within the mind. One can stop smoking and go along for years without even an urge to smoke. Yet upon smoking again only once or a few times, the very same groove that was known in the past is reactivated, and often strongly reasserts itself. In a day or two, the mind is almost convinced it cannot do without the tobacco it had not thought about for years.

The same kind of thought pattern exists around any habit. As we learn not to feed the demands of such a pattern, the feelings that the habit was protecting us from—feelings that are painful and difficult to face—emerge. By allowing these deeper feelings to surface and be released we come more fully into a place of clear perception and true aliveness.

Once on a radio interview, a woman asked the Sufi teacher Muzaffer Effendi why it was that she sometimes felt great love and expansiveness while meditating and at other times felt nothing. Effendi's answer was for the woman to look at what food she had been eating. The woman laughed. Unbeknownst to the teacher, she was the host of a cooking program on the radio station. The Sufi master went on to explain that he did not really mean literal food, but the thoughts and impressions the woman was ingesting. Such food could include complaints, backbiting, doubts, anger or resentment, or even the chaotic rhythm of another person in her life.

All of us partake of such kinds of food, consciously or unconsciously. We do so by our actions and speech, by entertaining thoughts or by absorbing and reflecting what comes to us from another. Learning what foods to ingest and what to avoid requires a great vigilance, an ability to allow impressions to pass through us without either resisting them or giving them life. A Buddhist teaching describes the proper attitude, gained via meditation, as realizing that passing impressions are akin to painting images on water. One can consciously allow all of our day-to-day impressions to simply dissolve.

Our natural and blissful mind is realized by paying attention to what we take in, ingesting what is inspiring and pure, and passing by what produces agitation or disharmony. It is by this vigilant work, however challenging, that our life fills with profound beauty, bringing healing to our souls and the world around us.

18
SPIRITUAL PRACTICES AS HELPFUL FRIENDS

The fulfillment of spiritual practice is diving deep within oneself; it is communicating with each atom of life existing in the whole world; it is realizing the real "I" in which is the fulfillment of life's purpose.[54]

The Yogi Milarepa

IN PREPARATION FOR MEDITATION, the practice of concentration on an object—such as an image in the mind's eye or a flower or crystal—serves as a "soap," cleansing impressions from the mind and heart. Concentration is a powerful tool for cutting through the distractions and illusions that keep us from our natural self.

The Hindu sage Vivekananda, who lived in the early 1900s and whose words of wisdom are still found daily within the major newspapers of India, taught that meditation does not have an ultimate value, in and of itself. It is simply a tool, allowing us to see beyond life's illusions and to open to true vision. It transforms the mind, taking it beyond its rigid pathways and deep furrows, opening it to natural clarity, spaciousness and unimpededness.

When we sit in concentration or meditation, and when we approach our lives as well as a meditation with open eyes, we are placing ourselves in the healing hands of a loving Divine physician. The doctor is very precise, giving us exactly the medicine we need to gain freedom and ecstasy, to open our hearts and remove all that stands between us and our natural being, our divine essence.

By spiritual practices, we develop a capacity that is useful each moment, freeing us from all that takes away our ease and our natural connection with life. As practices bring us to the natural state, they clear away confusion and murkiness in our thinking. Free from the mind's

---

[54] Hazrat Inayat Khan, *The Sufi Message of Hazrat Inayat Khan*, Vol. IV: Mental Purification (Geneva: International Sufi Movement, 1961), p. 156.

tendency towards opacity, doubt and hesitation, we find a tremendous increase in creativity and in the ability to appreciate all of life.

It is ironic that it takes so much practice and patience to come to our natural condition, which is peaceful and accepting, free of striving. Since this is our natural state, some spiritual schools downplay the need for practices, emphasizing the simple and radical acceptance of where we are at a given moment. Indeed there is a value in this, particularly because we have the tendency to make our spiritual practice into a project or obligation, and thereby miss its benefits. Yet it is possible that we can use spiritual practice in most easeful, beneficial and renewing ways, to provide fresh perception, breathing room and sacred rhythms within our busy lives. Practices can serve as protections from being continually bombarded with impressions and distractions, and can bring us closer to the natural world and its rhythms. They can help us to calm down, to restore balance and regain contact with our depths. Even the Dalai Lama, perhaps one of the most experienced spiritual practitioners on the planet, admits that he needs up to four hours of meditation each day to maintain clarity and his peaceful and consistently joyful state.

Spiritual practices eventually become like great friends on our path. As the plows and harrows of the psyche, they help us to become fertile and fruitful, open to new possibilities, creativity and beauty. Practices ultimately allow us to empty, soften and feel fully at home in our humanness. They bring us to stillness and receptivity, like the calm lake that can clearly reflect the light of the moon. In this condition, guidance and inspiration come to us, fulfilling an eternal covenant of loving care, sustenance and guidance that has been made with us: "*We shall show you Our signs on the horizon and within yourselves.*"[55]

In turn, inspiration and guidance yield fresh perception. Every experience becomes a living sacred manuscript, the gift of our life in an ever renewing, ever revealing creation, a sacred Emerald Earth.

[55] Qur'an, Sura 41, Verse 53.

INTRODUCTION TO PRACTICES

I once had the pleasure of hearing Paderewski in his own house. He began to play gently on his piano. Every note took him into a deeper and deeper ocean of music. Any meditative person could see clearly that he was so concentrated in what he did that he knew not where he was.[56]

SPIRITUAL PRACTICES, LIKE THE PLANTING OF SEEDS, unfold by a completely natural process, according to their own timing and course. Some of these seeds take a long time to reach fullness, yet the beauty they bring our lives is more valuable than anything in this world.

There are three essential types of practice described in this book, which we call concentration, contemplation and meditation. These practices are closely related, and there is a natural progression in practice from concentration to contemplation and meditation. There is also a fourth aspect, what we could call "non-meditation" or realization, which is the fruit of meditation, the effortless carrying of spiritual consciousness into our lives.

In *concentration*, we focus attention on an outer object or an image held in the mind's eye. Concentration is a most powerful practice for clearing old impressions and thereby taking the first steps toward the mind's natural state of clarity, luminosity and unimpededness.

In *contemplation*, we find some interplay between ourselves and the object that we focus upon. The word "contemplation" literally means the "joining of temples," and was applied to the practice of ancient sages who sought to align life events to the "templum" of the night sky and the constellational patterns they observed there. The contemplative practices we describe here use a parallel method—helping us to naturally align with cosmic rhythms and also to the "inner templum" or archetypes emerging from within—thereby bridging the soul and the world.

In *meditation* we experience a merging or unity with the object of our focus. Though usually first practiced in silence and solitude (even if only for a few minutes), meditation eventually becomes a practice of deep communication with all of life—both the silent life within and the world around us.

[56] Hazrat Inayat Khan, *The Sufi Message of Hazrat Inayat Khan*, Vol. IV: Mental Purification (Geneva: International Sufi Movement, 1961), p. 153.

Finally, in the "non-meditation" of *realization*, our practice bears fruit. We attain a most natural state of consciousness, of presence. It is a highly creative state, inspiring, renewing and healing.

Attaining the fullness of meditation is a lifetime's work. Often we do not recognize the actual fruits of our efforts, and it can be very easy to become disheartened in the absence of apparent results. A further story of the Buddhist sage Milarepa speaks of the challenge of perseverance with spiritual practice. Many years after his initial testing, even after spending years in solitary retreat, Milarepa began to question all his efforts. Ready to abandon his practice, he had a dream in which his teacher said, "My son, strengthen your will, have courage and work; you will furrow the hard and dry earth." Waking to ordinary consciousness, Milarepa wondered whether his dream had been true instruction or only his own wishful thinking. Ultimately, his inspiration and faith arose ever stronger, and he sang this song, one that is most appropriate to our explorations of the language of cultivation.

I cultivate the field of fundamentally non-discriminatory mind
with the manure and water of faith, and sow the seed of a pure heart.
The powerful thunder of my invocations reverberates,
and the rain of your blessings falls effortlessly.
Upon the oxen of a mind free from doubt
I put the yoke and plow of skillful means and wisdom.
Steadfastly I hold the reins without distraction.
Cracking the whip of effort, I break up the clods of the five poisons.
I cast away the stones of a defiled heart, and weed out all hypocrisy.
I cut the stalks and reap the fruit of action leading to liberation.
I fill the granary with the fruit of excellent instructions,
without the support of mental concepts.
This excellent grain, roasted and ground by the dakinis,
is the hermit's food for inner growth.
This is the meaning of my dream.
Realization does not arise out of words.
Understanding does not come from mere suggestions.
I urge all those who work for Enlightenment
to meditate with perseverance and effort.
Endurance and effort overcome the greatest of difficulties.
May there be no obstacles for those who seek Enlightenment.[57]

[57] Lobsang Lhalungpa, *The Life of Milarepa* (New York: Penguin Press, 1977), p. 113.

The Secret of the Breath

Breath... is a bridge between oneself and God; it is a rope for the Sufi, hanging down to earth, attached to the heavens. The Sufi climbs up by the help of this rope. In the Qur'anic language it is called Buraq, a steed which was sent to the Prophet for his journey to the heavens. Hindus call it Prana, which means life, but they picture it symbolically as a bird which is named in Sanskrit Garuda, on which rode Narayana, the Godhead.... Once one has touched the depths of her/his own being by the help of the breath then it becomes easy to become at one with all that exists on earth and in heaven.[58]

One of the most surprising effects of deep meditation, often quite contrary to initial experiences, is that we might begin to find ourselves feeling more sensitive and more agitated as we sit down to practice. In fact meditation does not really make us any more agitated, but it does make us more aware of what is buried beneath the surface of our mind and how unstable and unreliable our ordinary thinking is.

Traditional Buddhist teachings describe the meditator's experience of the mind to be first like water gushing through a gorge. Through meditation, the mind slows down and becomes like a wide and smoothly flowing river, and then eventually an ocean with gentle waves. Finally, when completely quiet, the mind is like a still lake, tranquil and able to take a clear reflection of the moon and stars.

Because of the mind's great instability and variability, there is nothing more beneficial than learning how to use our breathing as an aid to practice. A focus on breathing can be an immediate antidote to a restless mind, an anchor to a boat that is otherwise adrift on the sea.

The breath has been likened to a rope by which consciousness can be tied and stabilized, but also lifted: "Breath is the rope that takes us from this mortal plane to immortality, that saves us from the struggles and worries of this transitory life, and leads us to the happiness and joy and peace for which every soul longs."[59] Some aspect of breath will be used in most of the practices described in this book.

---

[58] Hazrat Inayat Khan, *The Sufi Message of Hazrat Inayat Khan*, Vol. XX: The Gathas. (Geneva: International Sufi Movement, 1982), p. 142.

[59] Hazrat Inayat Khan, Ibid, p. 142.

Practices—Preparing the Field of The Heart

Our first purpose in meditating is to clear away anything that brings unease, purifying and allowing ourselves to move towards the depths of our being. The practices in this section are catalysts for this preparation.

Practice #1: Tranquility Meditation—Dwelling in the Space between Thoughts

When a variety of thoughts come to mind, we think what appears is real and has some kind of material existence. It is as if we cannot see clearly because we are looking at a mirror's surface that needs cleaning. The view wipes it clear. For meditation to go well, it is important to have the right view and also one that has not been created by someone else. The Buddha taught different views and ways to meditate, but, in the final count, the actual view is the essential nature as it arises from our own mind. This is what is to be realized, and nothing else.[60]

Tranquility meditation, as practiced for twenty-five hundred years within the Buddhist tradition, is perhaps the simplest form of meditation practice. Outwardly it consists in simply resting the mind, not giving allegiance to any thought that arises.

1. Sit comfortably, in a chair or on a cushion on the floor, with your back fairly straight. Place your hands in your lap, palms facing up, right hand above left hand. Your eyes may be either half open or closed. For the duration of this practice, you simply breathe and allow your thoughts to pass naturally.

2. Do not resist any thought; however do not cultivate or adhere to any line of thinking. Just focus on your breathing, witnessing breathing in and out. To go deeper, you can especially pay attention to the exhalation and feel yourself dissolving, as if gently

---

[60] Karmapa Ogyen Trinley Dorje, *Music in the Sky: The Life, Art and Teachings of the 17th Karmapa* (Ithaca, NY: Snow Lion Publications), p. 176.

reaching out into space with the out-breath. Some variations are possible: You can count "one" on the inhalation and "two" on the exhalation, and then repeat again and again. Or you can count to ten, starting over if you lose count or when you reach ten.

3. No effort is made to change the rhythm or pattern of breathing. You can practice for five minutes and up to twenty minutes, sitting and simply observing, never judging your ability or progress. Just sit, and let yourself breathe, and feel all that you feel without consciously exploring why you feel anything.

4. Feel the freedom of allowing every thought, be it positive or negative, to liberate itself. Recognize the mind to be spacious, like an empty and clear blue sky. Each thought and feeling comes as a cloud, covering the light of the sky. Allow the thoughts and feelings to simply pass by, again and again revealing the clear sky. Feel an intensity, a sense of homecoming, as you rest from identifying with passing thoughts. Feel peace and freedom.

5. Try to practice at first for five minutes each day, using a timer and sticking to the practice until the time is up. If possible, gradually increase the time up to ten and then twenty minutes each day.

We have all kinds of thoughts—some inspiring, some that plague and obsess us. We do not have to give credence to the thoughts that agitate us. By this simple practice we are able to clarify and find spaciousness and freedom in our thinking.

When our minds are still, when we rest beyond ever-moving waves of emotion and mental constructs, we come to dwell in the wide space of the present moment. Fresh and open, we are free of the past and of concern for the future. With this reference point, we can perceive our thoughts as waves and, more importantly, recognize the space between the thoughts as revealing our true being, our Essence. Watching our thoughts and letting them simply pass, continually returning our focus to breathing, our whole being becomes tranquil.

As you watch your breathing, allow it to become refined, like a fine silken thread. Realize how breathing and thinking are interconnected, intricately and subtly woven together. Realize also the direct connection between the state of our mind and the rhythm of our breathing. The less agitation in the mind, the more refined and smooth our breathing becomes. The reverse is also true.

Ultimately, the gushing river of thought is calmed, and we rest deeply in the space between our thoughts. Here we truly realize our natural condition to *be* spaciousness and openness. Here the heart and mind join, and our thinking is ever "informed" by the depths of the heart. It is in this state that we are as a fertile field, open and ready to receive living seeds of new life.

Practice #2: Elemental Purification Breaths

The purification breathing practice we now describe is found in many spiritual traditions throughout the world. The practice works to gradually bring us into harmony with all the basic elements in nature and in our being. It purifies layers of impressions, confusion, doubt, fear and anxiety, allowing us to recognize the light of our true nature.

In this practice we are attuning ourselves to the elements of earth, water, fire, air and ether. The elements are living beings. They give shape to our minds and personalities. Attuning our own being to them helps us realize their existence within us. For example, if we wish for more of a sense of stability and peacefulness, we need only to meditate on the earth element in ourselves—in our bones and flesh. To connect with our fluid nature, and become better able to move around obstacles, we can meditate on water. Fire will bring us passion and intensity, air inspiration and freedom. Ether will help us feel communion, learn detachment and move beyond any sense of separateness. Each element has a spiritual correspondence: receiving stability and rootedness from the earth, nourished by the water of love, illumined by the rays of the sun, given clarity and quickened by the air of inspiration and permeated with the ether of Divine Presence, we are able to serve the awakening of consciousness around us, to bring forth an Emerald Earth, a life that is a true expression of beauty.

The secret of tapping into the power of the elements is in our honoring and respecting them as manifestations of the Divine. The Tibetan Buddhist tradition teaches that upon death we first experience the dissolution of the elements. We realize each as a garment, and experience a freedom in releasing from them. At the same time, while living on earth we honor the elements as the sacred supports of life, vehicles for healing, purification, freedom and clarity, transformation, inspiration and resorption into unity.

The elemental purification practice eventually becomes like a great friend on the spiritual path. Ideally practiced daily, it balances the elements in our beings, ever strengthening and cleansing us of hidden resistances, veils and negative impressions. It opens us to a vibrant life force, to creativity, and to the joy of our being.

Method for the Purification Breaths

At first we present a simple method for practice, then follow with more in-depth explorations and variations.

Begin with a deep exhalation, followed by a natural inhalation. Repeat.

EARTH element—breathe naturally in through the nose and out through the nose, five breaths contemplating the element of earth. Feel the healing power, firmness, patience, stability and sanity of the earth.

WATER element—breathe naturally in through the nose, out through the mouth. Five breaths. Feel purification, generosity, creativity, flowing around obstacles. Feel the love element flowing.

FIRE element—breathe naturally in through the mouth, out through the nose. Five breaths. Feel inspiration, passion, transmuting and transforming emotions.

AIR element—breathe naturally in through the mouth, out through the mouth. Five breaths. Contemplate freedom, lightness, ecstasy and joy.

ETHER element—breathe naturally in through the nose and out through the nose, a very subtle, refined breath. Five breaths. Feel a sense of union and interpenetration with all.

After you have become familiar with the basic practice, you may add some or all of the specific concentrations below, especially if you realize a need for more contact with particular elements.

Extended Concentration—The Earth Element

The contact with the earth element is very stabilizing and grounding. Native American elders have said that the loss of a sense of relationship and communion with the earth is the main cause of the prevalence of psychological imbalance in Western cultures. The early Christian hermits, often living alone for years in the desert, used a concentration on the earth's magnetism as a way of restoring their vitality.

If you have observed the way that iron filings line up in the presence of a magnet, you have a sense of how the earth's subtle magnetism works to restore our being. The earth is generous, ever offering us her gifts. Notice all the fruits, grains and flowers springing from the earth and the earth's capacity for bringing a seed to flower and fruition. The earth's wisdom and sanity restores us to our true nature—peaceful, generous, humble, and consistent.

1. Sitting or standing, feel yourself like tree with roots extending firmly and deeply into the earth. The earth breath is a process of filtering. Feel the great strength and magnetism of the earth. Breathe in through the nose and out through the nose, not forcing the breath in any way. Imagine drawing magnetism and healing power through the soles of your feet (if standing) or through the bottom of your spine (if sitting). Commune with the earth, and consciously channel the earth's magnetism to the parts of your body that are depleted.

2. As you breathe in and out, focus your awareness on the tip of the nose. The direction or inner feeling of the practice is horizontal and spreading, like the wide space of the earth itself. Imagine breathing in and out a yellow/gold color.

3. As you inhale, you are drawing electromagnetic energy up from the base of the spine, and celestial energy is coming down through the top of the head. It is an accordion effect, the magnetism of the earth rising, celestial energy and light descending. These two energies meet and collect in the heart.

4. As you exhale, let any polluted energy drain out of your tailbone down into the earth. With each inhalation and exhalation, recognize that you are drawing fresh and nurturing energy in, releasing toxins and filtering out heavy, dense energy from the base of the spine. The earth kindly accepts and transmutes the polluted energy. On the inhalation, remember yourself to be a part of life, your body made of the substance of the earth and part of the harmony of the natural world. As you exhale, release toxins back into the earth.

Meditating on the earth element develops and enhances patience, humility, endurance, stability and groundedness, and the ability to fashion and bring things to completion.

Extended Concentration — The Water Element

The breath of the water element is cleansing, purifying and revivifying. It unleashes creativity and helps us break free from habitual thinking patterns, allowing us to move around obstacles and maintain our forward momentum.

1. Concentrate on the purity of a crystal-clear lake or stream, high up in the mountains. Let yourself become the water, and let its purity, life energy and power flow into your immediate environment. Begin breathing in through the nose and out through the mouth. The focus is on the bridge of the nose. As you inhale, you draw breath up to the crown center, a few feet above the top of your head. With your inhalation you reach into the imaginal realms, into the source of the waters of life, clear and pure. Feel the part of your being that is pure, simple and immaculate, often represented by Mary, mother of Christ. As you exhale feel yourself under a fountain or waterfall of crystal-clear water.

2. Imagine being in a forest and a great profusion of water dripping off the leaves of the trees. Feel the purifying action of water clearing away all impurities, a baptism with water. Let the water permeate and open your being on all levels. Feel the gift of the water's surrender, and the resultant purification and revivifying action. Feel any stagnation being washed away, and the way that your connection with the water element can help you move around obstacles, and be inspired. Focus on the color light green.

Extended Concentration — The Fire Element

The purification of fire burns away impurities. It brings clarity and warmth. The fire is the force of truth that destroys hypocrisy, self-deception and dishonesty. See how you can turn anger into light; the victory of light over darkness. Let the fire kindle passion and intensity, overcoming dullness. Let your deepest desires intensify.

1. Breathe in through the mouth and out through the nose. Breathe in through the solar plexus and out the heart area. On the inhalation, feel as though you are fanning the embers in a fire in the solar plexus, burning away all that is dross, all that needs to be discarded. As you breathe in, concentrate on a red fire in the solar plexus. Pause a moment before the exhalation, turning attention to a sensitive point in the center of the rib cage (i.e., a few inches above the solar plexus). Here you imagine the red color transforming into gold. Breathe out the golden light from this higher point, allowing it to radiate in all directions.

2. A further development of this breath is to intensify the fanning of the fire in the solar plexus, breathing in the color red and then exhaling different colors of the light through all the higher chakras (i.e., the spiritual energy centers of the body): the gold in the heart becomes deep green in the throat, blue in the eyes, violet in the third eye and colorless diamond-like light in the crown. The direction of the fire breath is upwards.

As a consequence of this burning process we become more and more radiant. We breathe out a rainbow of light through the centers, especially emphasizing the golden light in the heart center and the cool, star-like light in the third eye. The radiance of the crown is diffused and widespread, opening to an infinite succession of further rainbows, each becoming more subtle, reaching into the clear light of bliss.

Extended Concentration—The Air Element

The breath of the air element puts us in touch with freedom, ecstasy and transcendence. The action of the air breath is that of scattering and dissolving the notion of an individual self, freeing the self from the confines of its boundaries and fixed notions and concepts.

1. Breathe in through the mouth and out through the mouth, with a focus above the crown of the head. On the inhalation, feel yourself buoyant and free, like a zephyr crossing a lake and lifting upwards. Feel all the spaces between the molecules of your being. On the exhalation, allow yourself to reach out beyond the boundaries of the body. Let your being disperse with the wind, and let your consciousness reach out into the cosmos.

2. Imagine yourself to be like a great eagle, with wings spread, high above a mountain. Feel the wind ruffling your feathers, blowing through all your pores. Feel the coolness and freshness of the air. Soar upwards on the currents of air.

3. Breath in and out a sky blue color. Enjoy a sense of vastness, visualizing vast landscapes—mountains, canyons or the starry night sky. Let every limitation be dispersed as you reach out into the galaxies. Release all concepts of being fixed or confined, and touch vastness.

The qualities of the air element are freedom from constraints, conventionality, conditioning, fixed and rigid thinking. Spaciousness and boundlessness allow new ways of perception and communication.

Extended Concentration — The Ether Element

The breath of the ether element is associated with the timeless and spaceless dimension of our being. The ether breath is very refined, almost imperceptible, in and out through the nose. With it is a feeling that our whole being is breathing. There is a sense of "being breathed" rather than breathing of our own volition. Colorless or smoky gray light is associated with this breath.

We often find ourselves dominated by an element — feeling matter-bound, overemotional, overcome by the fire of anger or the airy fluttering of thoughts. The ether element allows us to touch vastness but also embrace and balance the other elements.

Here, as you breathe in and out through the nose with a very refined breath, allow yourself to experience your being as open space, beyond any boundaries and concepts. Communicate, through your breathing, with all of life, not bounded by any sense of separate identity. Breathe spaciousness around any self-imposed constrictions, around physical and mental pain, allowing these to dissolve into the freshness of the moment.

As meditation deepens, as the mind's chatter and concerns settle down, a fragrance and taste come to us. The mysterious Beloved touches our life, and things that mattered so much are seen to mean very little. A Sufi hymn declares, "Smashing the bottle, nothing contains me." The "bottle" is our self-protection, our fear of relaxing into a natural state, of being foolish and accepting how little we really know of our own profound being. Allowing the universe in, on each breath, our exaggerated feelings of separateness — of being incomplete, unloved or somehow slighted by life — disappear in the light of truth.

Practice #3: Working with Light

Look up first, and when your eyes are charged with divine light, then when you cast your glance on the world of facts you will have a much clearer vision, the vision of reality.[61]

The following practices with light are best done in the early morning, at sunrise when the light is pure, clear and fresh.

1. Light in the Mind

With the eyes closed imagine looking directly into the sun. Imagine the light coming in through your eyes as you breathe in, flooding the optic nerve and the brain with light. As you inhale feel yourself drawing in luminous light. Allow this light to circulate and feel the optic nerve and brain drenched in light. Pause after you inhale to allow the whole brain to be filled with light. Then exhale and allow any impressions of darkness, doubt or heaviness to leave the mind. Become clear and illuminated with light. Extend the exhalation twice as long as the inhalation. As you work with this practice, you could repeat silently: "Thy light has illuminated the dark chambers of my mind."

2. Light in the Eyes

Inhale a clear and luminous light, celestial light, down through the crown from above the head. Thread this light down and breathe a crystalline light through the third eye, in the center of the forehead, and through the physical eyes. Feel the cleansing and purifying effect of the celestial light brought through the third eye, the locus of intuition and insight, and through your glance. Allow light to clarify your thinking and glance.

3. Light in the Heart

Wash your heart with light. Breathe light in and out of the heart. Allow the light to penetrate all the chambers of the heart,

[61] Hazrat Inayat Khan, *The Sufi Message of Hazrat Inayat Khan*, Vol. IV: Mental Purification (Geneva: International Sufi Movement, 1961), p. 27.

circulating, clearing away darkness, stagnation or ill will. Feel the heart to be a huge sun, radiating golden light. This is its natural state.

There is an image of Christ holding a lamp within his heart, protecting it from the winds and storms of life. This is our practice, protecting and safekeeping our inherent light-nature from obstructions, doubts, fears, and the tumult of our emotions, the storms of existence. Opacity is removed and the heart regains its inherent luminosity and clarity.

4. Transmutation of Energy

Breathe a gentle breath in through the solar plexus and out through the heart. As in the extended practice with the fire element, feel the transmutation of the fire of emotions in the solar plexus becoming a clear golden light radiating from the heart. Light raised in this way expresses our soul, rooted in love.

Prayer for Light

Oh God, give us Light in our hearts,
Light in our eyes, Light in our ears,
Light on our right, Light on our left
Light above us, Light beneath us,
Light before us, Light behind us;
and make Thou for us Light.
Light in our tongues, Light in our sinews
Light in our flesh, Light in our blood,
Light in our hair, Light in our intellects,
Light in our brains,
Light in our bodies, Light in our souls,
and magnify for us Light!
Oh God, bestow upon us Light! [62]

---

[62] A prayer of the Prophet Muhammad.

Practice #4: Facing a Bright Window

There is a reference in the writing of Zen Master Dogen to "facing a bright window." Dogen's metaphor gives a sense of an all-penetrating and all-clarifying light. We can turn our whole being towards light, opening ourselves to its purifying effect. While clouds come and go, the sun is still shining: the one unchanging light is constant through all that changes.

For this meditation, let yourself be bathed in the brilliance of light—every atom, every cell, every pore of your being suffused in light. Light is the ultimate object of contemplation. The image of light brings a feeling of waking up, of illumination.

We come to this life ignited by a spark from the one eternal light. We are part of the stars, and actually composed of stardust and light. Light is continuously streaming through the universe, offering us embrace, purification and guidance. Our true nature is connected to our light nature. What makes us become opaque, less transparent to light? What is the "bushel" that becomes a cover over our light?

There are many reasons we cannot experience light. We may hold to a sense of failure and disappointment, impressed by a faulty sense of self. We can be under a cloud of depression, even for many years, not knowing how to release impressions. We may not have enough faith to see that our seeming shortcomings and failures are integral stepping-stones in our unfolding. Or we may be so impressed by a disappointment that we feel we cannot "begin again." Whenever we dwell on all the limitations and shortcomings of ourselves and our world, we find endless problems. We are failing to see from a vaster, more spacious dimension, missing our birthright—the realization of our happiness, our true nature. Yet the divine spark is always waiting in our core to be rediscovered.

Failure does not matter in life. To a progressive person even a thousand failures do not matter. He keeps success before his view, and success is his even after a thousand failures. The greatest pity is when life comes to a standstill and does not move any further; a sensible person prefers death to such a life.[63]

Light loves truth and refuses anything false or artificial. When fac-

[63] Hazrat Inayat Khan, *Complete Sayings, Aphorisms* (New Lebanon, NY: Sufi Order Publications, 1978), p. 222.

ing light we are compelled to sift out any confused or distorted motives within us, anything that lacks clarity. We have nowhere to hide, and must bring into the light all that has been hidden. When light is thrown on what has been unconscious, new awareness comes. Light informs and fills us.

1. *Imagine yourself facing a bright window, the sun pouring through your being. Become transparent to light, allowing it to penetrate and blaze through you. Feel yourself like a crystal, wholly receptive to the light that fills all your pores. Body, mind and consciousness are bathed in light. If you feel any part of your being resisting the infusion of light, open up that area so it becomes wholly transparent, vulnerable, relieved of all masks — facing light, becoming light.*

2. *Touching light, bathing ourselves in light, we trigger a memory of having once been pure light before descending to the earthly plane. Here we are reactivating this identification with light. There is a great joy in this reawakening, in light overcoming negativity and fear, in our being completely transformed by the power and strength of brilliant light.*

The poet Rumi says: "Out beyond ideas of wrongdoing and rightdoing, there is a field, I will meet you there." Coming to this field, releasing blame of ourselves and others, we come to the Reality of this life, a world of mirrors meant only to express Love and to witness Beauty. Opening to this realization, accepting fully our beings and our unity with all, becomes the simple and yet radical step that changes us and changes our world.

Practice #5: Tuning the Heart

Throughout this next practice, breathe gently in and out of the spiritual heart chakra. This chakra is found in the center of the chest, behind an especially sensitive point about three inches above the solar plexus. After reading the instructions, continue these gentle breaths for five minutes, with eyes half opened or completely closed. Think of healing, opening and coming into tune.

We become out of tune when overworked and overtired, when we accumulate negative impressions and when anything weighs on our hearts. To bring our hearts into harmony, into tune, we first practice simply breathing in and out of the heart, being conscious of gradually releasing stored-up tension. Allow the muscle in the heart to soften, to melt. Again, for this to happen, we need to let ourselves and others off the hook, to forgive and release any impressions of having harmed or having been harmed by others, finding a state of natural repose and peace.

The tuning of our heart is a most gradual process. Being out of tune can mean we are responding to life from a lower pitch, much as we do when ill or upon first waking up in the morning. Anything that weighs upon us—grief, resentment, fatigue or frustration—may bring us to such a lower pitch.

Forgiving literally means "giving something before." This most radical and generous act may go against much of conventional psychology, which places a great emphasis on expressing feelings. Here, we can respect feelings and allow them to surface, gaining insight from them but not letting them rule our lives.

Forgiveness comes most easily when we realize that people hurt each other when they are acting out of their fear and suffering, and when they are asleep to the consequences of their actions. Everyone wants happiness. And while we may not always be able to honestly say we forgive, we can set a process in motion by our intention, our desire to move beyond whatever it was that hurt. By this, we are letting ourselves (and one or more other souls) out of a prison. We come to realize that there is really no one to blame for anything that takes place in our lives. Forgiveness is a radical and courageous step that changes us and our world. As layers of protection, drop away, and as we remember our unity with all, we are relieved of our confusion, doubt and sense of alienation.

To begin to tune our hearts, we may be able to do nothing more than make an intention to let go and release the past. In fact, true letting go and forgiveness are divine gifts, and these come in their own time, often when we do not expect them. At the same time, our simple act of intention is crucial to setting into motion a process that brings not only forgiveness but also satisfaction and peace, and yields a powerful opening to the bounty and gifts provided by unseen sources.

Practice #6: Mystic Concentration

Usually, without being aware of it, we try to change something other than ourselves; we try to order things outside of ourselves. But it is impossible to organize things if you yourself are not in order. When you do things in the right way, at the right time, everything else will be organized. You are the boss. When the boss is sleeping, everyone is sleeping. When the boss is doing something right, everyone will do everything right, and at the right time.[64]

There is an irony in our unfolding. To become truly natural and creative, we must learn intense discipline and concentration. Like the master musician, we must first learn scales before improvising. This development of concentration is the secret of success in any endeavor.

In some part of our life, most of us know something of the power and freedom that comes from concentration. Children naturally know the intensity of concentration, if not its duration. When we are fully absorbed in some work, in carpentry, music or dance, we experience natural concentration, a wonderful freshness and clarity, and an emancipation from time. Yet for many people the natural sense of concentration has been lost. It is as if we have fallen off a horse, and, instead of getting back on, have been sidetracked. Part of spiritual awakening is learning again how to concentrate.

Concentration methods are demanding. The mind, like a restless horse, balks at being disciplined. Remembering the goal can help, for the natural state of concentration is not rigid—it leaves enough room for us to be responsive and receptive to the life around us.

Just as physical exertion does for the body, concentration both exercises the mind and eventually brings it to a state of ease. Concentration also works as a soap, cleansing the mind of layers of past impressions, restoring a natural and spacious condition of peace and clarity. Through simple concentration practices, we also gain the great power to turn our mind in the direction we wish.

Developed and used properly, without rigidity, concentration becomes our true ally, a boat that carries us through life's stormy waters, through the distractions that pull at us from every side. A truly concentrated mind is ever creative and can shape a most beautiful life, one that is much less complicated and more satisfying.

While we first focus on a flower or crystal to develop concentra-

[64] Shunyru Suzuki, *Zen Mind, Beginner's Mind* (New York, Weatherhill), pp. 27-28.

tion, the ultimate goal is to apply the practice to every aspect of our life. The word "concentration" comes from the Latin, *concentrum*, meaning "with center." The secret of the deepest concentration, in any activity, is to center ourselves on whatever we do, and to infuse everything, even the most mundane of activities, with love. In Rumi's words, "Circle what you love; the circling comes from the center."

Focus on an External Object

Concentration is like making a pin stand on the tip of a finger, which has always a tendency to fall. The nature of the mind is such that it creates a thought and throws it over for another thought to take its place. This makes it difficult to concentrate upon one object steadily.[65]

1. Place some beautiful object at eye level in front of you—a flower, a vase, a crystal or a gem. Hold your glance upon the object without wavering, and be aware of your breath. Breathe naturally and don't attempt to control the breath. Let your thoughts pass without giving too much attention to them, and keep bringing your attention back to the object of concentration as it wavers.

2. Though you must steady your glance, allow it to soften. As your mind wanders, your glance will also. Keep coming back to the object. Be aware of detail, but only enough to maintain an interest in the object. Let your thoughts and feelings pass by, considering them as background, and don't allow them to take precedence over the object of concentration.

3. As you develop concentration, the object of your concentration will begin to appear very differently. A richness in color or the beauty of detail may become more apparent. Gradually you will sense a deeper reality beyond the physical appearance. The object will seem suspended in space, and the richness of its presence will manifest.

4. Toward the end of this practice, close your eyes and visualize the object internally. Hold the concentration on the image. As the image begins to fade, repeatedly "create" the image in your mind's eye.

5. Start with five minutes of practice, and then gradually build

[65] Hazrat Inayat Khan, unpublished papers

your concentration to ten or fifteen minutes. Practice until you feel that your powers of concentration have carried over into other aspects of your life, strengthening your will and your ability to focus.

Practice #7: A Breathing Practice for Deep Concentration

This breathing practice is especially effective in directing the mind towards healthy forms of concentration. This is most necessary, because we have an almost uncanny ability to concentrate on negative thoughts, judgments, doubts and fear, and we have to train ourselves to focus on what brings us joy and peace.

To return to a metaphor we used earlier in the book, our mind is like a phonograph record, and the lines engraved on this record are continually resounding. Even the cells of our bodies serve in the process, storing the thought patterns represented by these lines. Our very postures, movements and sensations continually trigger the deep lines of memory, repeating to us all that is recorded. By the practice we will describe here, we are forging new pathways in our minds, lifting consciousness beyond the engraved lines that would otherwise hold sway upon us.

This breathing practice takes us beyond discursive thinking to intuition and feeling, and yields a powerful radiance and harmonious rhythm in our being. It opens all the channels of breath from the base of the spine to the crown—especially the energy centers at the heart, throat, third eye (center of the brow) and crown (at the top of the head). It also restores the natural balance of masculine and feminine elements within us, the sun (right) and moon (left) sides of our being.

1. Sitting erect, place the thumb of your right hand under your chin, and put the middle finger of the right hand on the right nostril. When instructed, this finger will close off the right nostril. Position the left thumb over the left nostril in the same way. The rest of the fingers of your left hand should gently wrap around your right fingers.

2. When instructed to hold the breath, gently close both of the nostrils. You will be breathing in and out to a certain count, holding the breath for twice the length of the inhalation and exhalation.

3. Close your eyes, and take a deep exhalation, gently releasing the air out of your abdomen and lungs. Let your inhalation be completely natural and unforced. Repeat. Repeat again and, after the third exhalation, close your right nostril and breathe naturally into the left nostril, mentally counting to four. Close both nostrils and hold your breath for a count of eight. Now release your finger from your right nostril and breathe out to a count of four. Ideally, the count corresponds to the rhythm of the heartbeat.

4. Repeat, two more cycles, in left four, hold eight, out the right four.

5. Now reverse the process, this time breathing in through the right nostril to a count of four, holding a count of eight and breathing out the left nostril to a count of four. Again repeat this sequence for another two cycles.

6. Now breathe in through both nostrils to a count of four, and here focus deeply within and up into the third eye, (the chakra in the center of the forehead, its center immediately above the palate). Do not strain. Hold a count of eight, and then exhale out of both nostrils to a count of four. Now again repeat this two more times. On the last exhalation, breathe out the third eye, the front of the throat and the heart center (in the center of the chest).

Relax. When you are breathing in on the left, you are focusing on the female or receptive side. On the right, the emphasis is on the male or expressive side. When you breathe through both nostrils, you are interweaving the energies of the two sides.

Summary:
In left nostril four, hold eight, out right nostril four (three times)
In right nostril four, hold eight, out left nostril four (three times)
In both nostrils four, hold eight, out both four (three times)

Practice #8: Becoming Transparent to Light

My mind is full of light, my heart is full of light, my soul is full of light, my limbs are full of light.

— Sufi Alayhi

To remain transparent to light is a commitment to our true nature. It means the willingness to open and empty ourselves of darkness, of our resistance, of the barriers we have to being vulnerable. By this we come to serve our depths, our true and radiant nature.

Imagine first facing a very bright light. Let the light pour in and penetrate your being. Be like a crystal, transparent to light, passive to the action of this light illuminating all the dark recesses of your being. Feel receptive and totally empty of any clouds of preconceptions, opinions, prejudices, impressions: any opacity is transformed into transparency; allow light to pass through you as you clear out old ways of sclerosed thinking. Feel aligned to this higher order of light and let its clarity and pitch inform you. Let any opacity dissolve as you open more fully and commune with brilliant and spacious light. If it is helpful, look at a crystal for a few moments, and then close your eyes and imagine entering the crystal. Feel light passing through you.

The vibration or pitch of light is transforming. When we are transparent to light we lose our sclerosed sense of self. Every atom of our being is informed with light, and this produces a sense of deep and ecstatic communion with the source of light.

PART III: Touching the Ground of Being

Part III describes the soul's homecoming, a return to the ground of Being, our true identity. It explains how this inner experience informs our vision, so that we truly see the sacred, the imprint and mirror of the Absolute, in every aspect and moment of life.

Introduction: Our Essence

To the mind that is still,
The whole universe surrenders
—Lao Tzu

OUR ESSENCE—the ever-living and limitless ground of being—is our true home. It is a spacious, clear field, free from the limitations of personal impressions, beliefs, and habitual thinking. The ground of being encompasses all, interpenetrates all. It is like the lotus plant, with flowers floating on the surface, appearing as separate but completely connected below the surface. At the ground of being, we realize ourselves wholly united with and connected to all of life.

In a culture that places great emphasis on outer accomplishment, the kinds of meditation that bring us to the ground of being are not so easily valued. Meditative logic turns the world upside down, helping us to realize that, at certain crucial moments, our busy pursuits in all directions may yield nothing. It is the single-minded pursuit of our essence that brings everything of true value to our lives.

What is gained in the kinds of deep meditation presented in this section reverberates in the life around us. In fact, touching the ground of being is the essential key to realizing an "Emerald Earth." In our language, it is the attainment of a clear and fertile field made ready by diligent practice. Coming home to this ground clarifies our perception, allowing us to embrace life's dream with compassion and deep peace.

By deep meditation we are truly able to see the "signs on the horizon and inside of ourselves," to realize that this precious dream life exists to manifest splendor. By the opening afforded by our practice, we begin to experience the truth that each moment is a unique, creative and poetic expression of a loving, intelligent and ever-guiding Universe.

19
THE ESSENCE OF BEING

There is a stage at which, by touching a particular phase of existence, one feels above the limitations of life, and is given that power and peace and freedom, light and life, which belong to the source of all beings.... It is just like touching the Presence of God, when one's consciousness has become so light and so liberated and free that it can raise itself and dive and touch the depths of one's being. In other words, in that moment of supreme exaltation one is not only united with the source of all beings, but dissolved in it; for the source is one's self.[66]

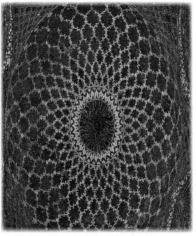

Ceiling of the red sandstone mosque at the Taj Mahal, Agra, India

Z EN ABBOT JOHN DAIDO LOORI TELLS ABOUT HIS INITIAL STRUGGLES with the practice of "sitting Zen." He had spent a few years practicing with—at least in his view—no apparent success in changing his consciousness or getting beyond habitual mental patterns. Finally, in the middle of a very intensive meditation retreat, Daido Loori decided that he had just had enough. He was intent on walking out of the meditation hall and, once and for all, leaving Zen behind.

Daido Loori's plan was that, during a break in the retreat, he would quietly disappear. As he stepped out of the Zendo and turned toward the parking lot, an assistant teacher, thinking that the student had simply made a wrong turn, pointed in the opposite direction. He turned Daido Loori around, away from the parking lot and towards the rest of the group who were standing in a courtyard for their break between practices.

Too embarrassed to leave, Daido Loori went back inside. In a rather desperate state he told his teacher, stately Hakuyu Taizan Maezumi, that his legs hurt from all the sitting, and that he didn't know how he could continue. The compassionate teacher's solution was simple yet firm. He said, "Just sit!" Daido Lori sat down, and, almost

[66] Hazrat Inayat Khan , *The Sufi Message of Hazrat Inayat Khan,* Vol. IV: Mental Purification (Geneva: International Sufi Movement, 1961), p. 115.

instantaneously, entered a state of deep absorption—a timeless state of samadhi. The next thing he knew he was listening to the pleasing sounds of meal preparation. A whole day had passed in painless and effortless meditation.

Contact with our spiritual depths often does come as a gift, when we have given up our hope of its attainment. However long it takes, it is important to recognize that practice yields fruits. As one tradition teaches, "If you sit long enough at a doorstep, sooner or later the owner of the house will appear." In other words, as a result of meditation, consciousness eventually spills over the boundaries of our assumed identity. The result is that deeper states of being and inner revelation begin to open to us. When this happens, we are never again the same. In the words of Hazrat Inayat Khan,

> *The soul receives a kind of illumination which is like a torch lighting another light; this inner life, touching the consciousness, produces a sort of illumination which makes our life clear. Every moment after this experience is unveiled... It charges one's life with new life and new light.*[67]

---

[67] Hazrat Inayat Khan, *The Sufi Message of Hazrat Inayat Khan*, Vol. IV: Mental Purification (Geneva: International Sufi Movement, 1961), p. 202.

20
REDISCOVERING INNER SENSES

That inner part [of life] is sound, that inner part is light; and when one gets in touch with this sound and this light, then one knows that language which is the language of heaven, a language which is expressive of the past, the present and the future, a language which reveals the secret and character of nature, a language which is receiving and giving that divine message which the prophets have tried at times to reveal.[68]

WE OFTEN MEET LIFE with a vision that is colored by our thoughts and concerns. With deep meditation, the experience of our ordinary senses becomes most extraordinary — clear, inspiring and even revelatory. Eventually deeper and more subtle senses reveal themselves.

When the outer senses are closed, our inner being can open up. When outer sight and hearing are de-emphasized, we discover and tune in to the "eyes and ears of the heart." The meditations here will help reveal to us this rich inner world, and provide us with a means of integrating this revelation with the rest of our experience.

In deep meditation, the first new revelations of the senses come as inner sound. We feel the vibration of the cave of our heart, heralding an opening to the eternal, a place of peace and tranquility; and a healing balm permeates and echoes through our being.

As sound deepens, a subtle chemistry and an inner landscape reveal themselves. With conscious breathing, we learn to nourish and cultivate, to water and make fertile this inner landscape of our being. As the science of yoga describes, we discover inner channels and chambers that come alive as subtle breath reaches and irrigates them.

[68] Hazrat Inayat Khan, *The Sufi Message of Hazrat Inayat Khan*, Vol. II: The Mysticism of Sound (Geneva: International Sufi Movement, 1962), pp. 133-34.

Akin to inner sound is a corresponding experience of inner light. As we withdraw from our tendency to look outside, we experience light emerging from within. Inner light shines within the subtle energy and nerve centers, clarifying and bringing forth a knowledge that has been dormant, as if awaiting its rediscovery. Pir Vilayat calls this *protocrytic* knowledge, emphasizing its uniqueness and independence from any outside information or experience.

Inner light emerges from what has appeared as emptiness. It is luminous and black, and is absolutely potent and fertile. From it wells up a spring of creativity and insight, infusing all of our being. This experience is profound, a gentle stream of exquisite beauty and light that settles our inner chatter and anxiety. We experience a natural happiness, lightness and transparency, and these are felt to be deeply connected to the energy, intelligence and essence of life itself.

A further subtle sense arises, that of ambrosia, tangible and fragrant. This heralds ecstasy, the intoxication coming from drinking the wine of unity. It is said that the prophet Abraham was thus inebriated, every pore of his being saturated with Divine presence and fragrance. In this state, the Indian goddess Saraswati dances and renews the earth, the rivers, the sciences and the arts. In awe and profound humility, we realize ourselves as essential Love, as the single taste and presence of Mystery. We feel, in our depths, that we are at home in the Holy Mystery our soul has sought and longed for.

21
THE BACKWARD STEP

The secret of happiness is hidden under the veil of spiritual knowledge. And spiritual knowledge is nothing but this: that there is a constant longing in the heart of the human to have something of its origin, to experience something of its original state, the state of peace and joy which has been disturbed, and yet is sought after throughout its whole life, and never can cease

to be sought after until the real source has at length been realized. What was it in the wilderness that gave peace and joy? What was it that came to us in the forest, the solitude? In either case it was nothing else but the depth of our own life, which is silent like the depths of the great sea, so silent and still.[69]

We turn in every outer direction seeking satisfaction, peace and joy, until eventually we find what we have been searching for in our own hearts. To find our depths, we have to take a "backward step," an inner pilgrimage, via some form of meditation.

Looking from the outside, and as one begins, meditation can appear to be very boring. In truth, sitting in silence will eventually bring forth an infinite richness and fullness that we could never have dreamed possible. These words of the Buddhist sage Longchenpa attest to this:

Listen, vajra being, now practice correctly. When meditating on pure, unborn reality, what appears is neither concretized nor latched onto. Because what appears never becomes what it appears to be and is intrinsically free. In this bliss which, in its very being, is free from concepts, there is nothing to objectify, seek or contrive with body, speech or mind. There is nothing to focus on or characterize. Just relax in the reality of this blissful self-generating pristine awareness. This is the deep experi-

[69] Hazrat Inayat Khan, *The Sufi Message of Hazrat Inayat Khan*, Vol. VII: In An Eastern Rose Garden (London, International Sufi Movement, 1962), pp. 42-43.

ence of self-originating clear light. This is the activity, in its deepest sense, of the majestic creativity which fashions everything.[70]

Removing the obstacles that prevent us from experiencing the depths of meditation requires, at least at first, placing ourselves in a situation in which we can truly relax. Be it for a few days or even a few hours, being free from the demands of the world and from our own psyches allows us to reconnect with the creative core of our being.

The attainment of deep meditation is akin to floating on water and being effortlessly buoyed up. For the time of meditation, we give up striving, and simply become like an empty cup. We open to receive, as if effortlessly mining a mysterious jewel.

However simple, deepening relaxation is a great challenge. It requires us to know and to train our surface minds and our emotions. It confronts us with our restlessness and struggles, with the mind's rebellion and its tentacle-like grasping. Gradually, through the practices that continually return attention to the breath or to another object of concentration, the mind releases its grip. In the depths of silence and stillness we touch the wellsprings of life, "the majestic creativity which fashions everything."

Having this deep experience is the key to our transformed vision and to continually perceiving creative beauty—an Emerald Earth. Thomas Merton called it the realization of *le point vierge*, "the virgin point." He described it as first an experience of pure nothingness and poverty, bringing a sense of freedom from illusions, as "pure diamond, blazing with the invisible light of heaven."[71] It was this experience that allowed Merton to realize, much to his own surprise, that the life and the people around him were truly sacred. All of a sudden, all the meaning Merton had sought in solitary contemplation was before him in the everyday world, the world that he had at one time rejected (see pages 146-48 below).

---

[70] Longchenpa, *You Are the Eyes of the World*, trans. K. Lipman and M. Petersen (Ithaca, NY: Snow Lion Publications, 2000), p. 36.

[71] Merton's description of *le point verge* is found in *Conjectures of a Guilty Bystander* (New York, Doubleday, 1966), p. 142.

Practices — Touching the Ground of Being

The practices related to the ground of being help to turn consciousness within, so that we can experience the deepest levels of meditation. They release us from the everyday impressions that continually pull us from our deepest identity. While some of these practices here are often used for extended periods of spiritual retreat, they are also very useful as daily meditations, giving us greater perspective and clarity.

> *You should be able to untether yourself from the world and set yourself free, loosing all the fine strings and strands of tension that bind you, by sight, by sound, by thought, to the presence of other[s].... We do not go into the desert [of solitude] in order to escape people but to learn how to find them, we do not leave them in order to have nothing more to do with them, but in order to find out how to do them the most good.*[72]

Practice #9: Progressive Relaxation

Part A: Working with the Body

This practice encourages deep relaxation of both the body and mind. Sitting comfortably or lying down, begin by relaxing the extremities of your body, tensing the various muscles momentarily and then releasing them. Push a bit on the exhalation and, as you do, tense the body part you are concentrating on. As you inhale, relax and breathe completely and naturally. Work slowly and gradually.

Begin with the thumbs and big toes. Tense and relax.

Next, the forefingers and second toes. Tense and relax.

Gradually work through the rest of the fingers and the corresponding toes. Tense and relax.

Now tense and relax all of the fingers and toes simultaneously.

Palms of the hands and the soles of the feet. Tense and relax.

Calves and forearms. Tense and relax.

Elbows and knees. Tense and relax.

Upper arms and thighs. Tense and relax.

---

[72] Thomas Merton, *New Seeds of Contemplation* (New York: New Directions, 1961), p. 80-81.

Shoulders and hips. Tense and relax.

Bottom of the spine and the area around the genitals. Tense and relax.

Lower back and abdomen. Tense and relax.

The stomach and the lower back. Tense and relax.

The solar plexus and the center of the back. Tense and relax.

The upper back and the center of the chest. Tense and relax.

The shoulder blades and collarbone area. Tense and relax.

Roll the shoulders and release tension here.

The neck. Tense and relax, including the area at the base and the front of the neck.

Now the jaw. Draw the cheeks back as you tense the jaw. Relax.

Now relax the lips, the bridge of the nose, the eyes, the eyebrows and the temples. There is usually much tension in these areas, so go slowly and release as much of the tightness as you can. Take time to relax and breathe deeply.

Now the forehead. Tense and relax.

Finally, the top of the head. You will find, through some experimenting, that you can use a muscle in the top of the head to push the brain up against the skull. Tense and relax.

Part B: Working With the Mind

Begin the second phase by reflecting back to an earlier time this day. Choose a pleasant moment, one that does not have a tense or negative tone. Try to visualize this moment, holding an image of it momentarily in your mind's eye.

Now go back a week. Hold the image momentarily.

Now go back about a month. The further back you go, the more time it may take to remember the circumstances and the experience. Take your time and keep the focus until you arrive at a memory you can briefly contemplate.

Now back a year.

Five years.

Ten years.

Twenty years.

Go back to your childhood.

Try to recall a memory of babyhood.

Now reflect upon your being in the womb.

Be receptive to the slightest memory or physical sensations.

Sit in meditation for a few moments to conclude this practice. You might imagine yourself as being deep under water, and each thought as a bubble that rises up and is dispersed. To conclude, feel a buoyancy, remaining in a threshold state for a few minutes.

Practice #10: Insight Meditation

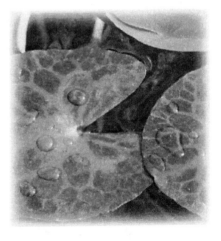

To live from our true being requires us to see beyond layers of identity that have accrued over the course of our lives. To adapt to this world we have become alienated from many of our own true feelings, our true desires, and our natural way of being. Our limitless souls have accepted a narrowed-down description of self and reality. And while feeling human limitation brings a sense of humility, it can also result in a loss of a sense of purpose, robbing us of our freedom and bliss.

The insight meditation we present here is one of the most effective practices for helping us to come back to our true nature. It is simple and yet powerful in its ability to challenge and dissolve our mistaken assumptions, assessments, judgments, opinions, and false identifications. It is a practice that helps us truly recognize life's fleeting nature, remembering that we are visitors here for a brief time, part of a much longer journey. As the revered Tibetan teacher Kalu Rinpoche described, it allows a most necessary perception of a "crack in the vessel" of our seemingly solid and stable—in fact imprisoning—picture of our lives and ourselves.

In the course of this practice, we welcome release from mechanical reactions and negative habits of thinking. As Christ said, we cannot put new wine into old wineskins: here we allow ourselves, through the action of meditation, to be purified and swept clean of false assumptions and ways of being. In the language of this book, we are clearing the old roots, stems and rocks of past experience so that the seeds of our potential may unfurl.

Through this practice, we dig deeply, finding the hidden jewels of our potential and our wisdom. Stepping back, calling a halt and allowing the din and static of our lives to settle and dissipate, we touch unfathomable peace and an ever-rising wellspring of life energy.

The method we present here draws upon two complementary perspectives, found in both Vajrayana Buddhism and the Sufi tradition. When formally offered, the practice begins with a teacher "pointing out" certain inconsistencies and curious facts about our human condition, identity and predicaments. By seeing the contradictions in our distorted and one-sided views of life, we open to new vistas.

Instructions for Practice

We begin by sitting comfortably, on a chair or cushion. The spine should be as straight as possible, though not stiff. Eyes can be closed, with the glance softened, attention turned upwards to the third eye point, in the center of the brow. Alternatively, the eyes can be half opened with the gaze lowered slightly, not focusing on external objects. During the practice there will be times when attention will be shifted towards the heart chakra, a few inches above the solar plexus, in the center of the chest.

Clearly set an intention to touch the truth of your being, to disengage from misconceptions and misidentifications of body, emotions, mind, perception, or consciousness. Allow yourself the joy of homecoming, of letting go and sinking deeper and deeper into the ground of your being. Touch the place of peace and luminous intelligence, the "clear light of bliss." Without limiting your sense of identity, reach out into the vastness or breadth of your being, and reach into the deepest depths of your heart. Allow your vantage point to shift from an emphasis on survival to an expansive and unconstrained mode of being. Identify yourself as all of life, both within and without.

Freedom from Form

Begin to examine form. Ask yourself, "Am I my body? Am I my physical form?" Usually we take it for granted that our body and identity are one. Yet, while the body is intended to be an instrument of our being, it has a will of its own. We know this whenever we try to exercise control over the body, and see how it resists, much as a wild horse balks at attempts to taming.

Sitting still, we concentrate on dissolving form in order to experience what is behind it. We look at our identification with our body, and our sense of the body as being separate from other bodies. We reflect on our illusory sense of possession of our body, and how this possession parallels the mistaken sense of ownership of other forms or objects, such as land, houses, clothing, books, etc., within the physical universe. In truth we possess nothing, and yet, in touch with the ultimate reality behind all forms, we possess everything.

Matter, appearing solid, is not, and everything about our own "form" is ultimately subject to change and dissolution. So here we recognize that our body will quickly decompose, and that letting go of our present identification gives us a glimpse of the part of us that never dies.

Allow yourself, with each exhalation, to experience the dissolution of form. In your consciousness, let the body and all of the physical universe simply dissolve. Realize that the body is continually dying and being renewed, and sense the truth that behind your name and form you exist as the pure consciousness that permeates all the universe.

Freedom from Emotion

Next, observe emotions. These include the whole spectrum of feelings—splendor, nostalgia, joy, exhilaration, anger, hurt, betrayal, inadequacy, etc. Experience emotions to be like passing clouds. Recognize without judgment the strong attachment we have to our emotions, and the truth that we are not our emotions. Feel the charge around emotions dissolving, while looking at the situations where emotions and feelings are especially stirred. See yourself gaining freedom in these situations, especially allowing the strongest negative feelings and reactions to melt away. Real-

ize that your strong aversions to situations or people are just not worth their cost, and affirm your intention not to be imprisoned by these. Let negative emotions be washed in cool rainwater, and feel the tremendous relief and freedom this brings. Allow deeper feelings of love and peace to emerge naturally.

Freedom from Perception

By "perception" we refer to all the experience of life through our senses. Our senses are gifts, each offering us a form of beauty, and each able to bring us towards our deepest nature. Yet our senses can also overwhelm us, as they tend to do when we are drawn in many directions, bombarded by too much sensory input.

Here, recognize the pull of senses. Be a witness to the way your eyes and ears, and in fact all your senses, are drawn to stimuli in the world. Without any fight or resistance, simply relax each time you feel your senses pulling you. Rest in a passive state of witnessing.

Freedom from Ordinary Thinking

Going deeper, recognize what we call mind, and our assumed continuity of thoughts, to actually be habits of thought—mental constructs, assumptions and expectations. These actually cover our awareness that mind truly is a clear and unhindered luminosity, an ever-arising fresh fountain of inspiration. Here we let go of all that we think we know, of our assessments of how things are, of what is good, bad, wrong and right. We allow the solid sense of mind to become fluid, dissolving into a state of unknowing, clear and empty of any residue of stagnant thoughts.

Freedom from Consciousness

Finally, reflect on consciousness, and see that it is a kind of funneling down of vast awareness into a focal point. This funneling down is a necessary and useful phenomenon, allowing us to develop skills for survival, adaptation and evolution. Yet here we recognize that our basic nature is spacious and vast. This narrowing action can be relaxed as we allow our consciousness to expand beyond the limited sense of "self," ultimately realizing ourselves to be united with the whole backdrop of existence.

By this practice, we actualize a knowledge expressed by Buddha, i.e., that consciousness is both a flame and the fuel for its own fire. The more consciousness focuses on the world, the more the world demands its attention. Here consciousness becomes free, extending beyond the world of time and variety into vastness and touching the unchanging realm of being.

Practice #11: Uncreated Light

Light is our very essence. The soul knows its true nature as light, and this becomes a certainty to us within deep meditation. Contemplating light, we reconnect with our original nature.

Using insight meditation (Practice #10) as a starting point, we enter through the heart to the realm of uncreated or "luminous black light." Here we are connecting with the light of intelligence, beyond form and objects, beyond radiant "created" light or the light of the physical aura. The scaffolding of our ego becomes more transparent. We see how we are continually emerging, moment by moment, from an ocean of uncreated light. We realize that we vitalize the environment with the light of our souls. The light of distant stars and galaxies concentrates within us and radiates outwardly. Our bodies are literally made of stardust, our minds and souls of the pristine intelligence and light of the universe.

This "black light" we speak of us is a clarity, a bliss-filled emptiness, a purity that is ours but impersonal. Dwelling in luminous uncreated light, we touch our true nature. The Zen Buddhist tradition speaks here of connection with our "original face," far different from the part of our being that is temporally projected into space and time. From our hearts radiates pure luminosity, the ecstasy of light.

Practice #12: Light upon a Light

We can dive into the heart like a deep sea diver, and when we do we reach a place of connection with all beings. Here with awareness of the black and luminous light, we feel ourselves expand, merge and dwell in a most exquisite sense of presence, a homecoming of our soul with the Soul of all.

As an extension of the meditation on uncreated light (Practice #11), from this deep place we bring our awareness right up the spine, through the deep blue light in the third eye and then

97

up above the crown. Here we experience the clear light of intelligence, again the realization of the part of us that has existed since before time and beyond our ordinary sense of becoming. This is the light behind the created universe, a "place" that we know most intimately, timeless and changeless, vast and even beyond any conceptions of space.

As we explore further this landscape of the soul, the light from above the crown descends and meets the light in the solar plexus. We experience the merging of two lights. This merging is an internal representation of the fulfillment of our purpose for existing, a marriage of the light of the heavens and the earth, and an infusing of our being with presence, blessing and luminosity. The rising light meets a descending light and becomes a "light upon a light." We experience ourselves as pure, luminous consciousness, aware of both a vast ocean of light and our home within this ocean as a unique and transparent vessel of light.

The experience here, which began with a dis-identification with all that is transient, again joins us with the world. Our being becomes a mantle of light. This experience of "light upon light" fills the life around us, communicating energy, ecstasy and intelligence.

PART IV: Sowing the Seeds of the Emerald Earth

Part IV describes the impregnation of our being with the seeds of awakening, and the effect of this on the life around us. It emphasizes "meditation in life," using intention and creative vision to enhance both inner and outer life.

Introduction: Shifting Directions in Meditation

And when the mind becomes smooth by unlearning and by digging out all impressions, of good and bad, of right and wrong, then the ground of the heart becomes as cultivated ground, just as the land does after plowing. All the old stumps and roots and pebbles and rocks are taken off, and it is made into ground which is now ready for the sowing of the seed.[73]

Up to this point we have been presenting meditations that have to do with stepping back from life, clearing away all that blocks our experience of our eternal dimension, the essence of our being. Now the direction of meditation will shift.

As we noted, spiritually oriented people often feel quite at home with solitary meditations and find it difficult to view their waking experience as an equally worthy object of practice. Indeed, once we make contact with freedom, vastness and splendor in meditation, it may be hard for us to see why we should fully invest the ordinary world with our attention. But this is a great mistake, and can result in the loss of a most precious opportunity, one that may never again come our way.

There are many illustrations in spiritual lore of the seeker who leaves the world behind for the inner quest, eventually to realize that spirituality is to be found in everyday experience. One example is that of Nikos Kazantzakis, described earlier. Another is found in Somerset Maughan's novel *The Razor's Edge*, in which the main character's quest leads him away from ordinary life in pursuit of spiritual knowledge. Ultimately the seeker discovers meaningfulness in the very life he had tried to leave behind.

Having prepared the soil of our being, clearing our mind and heart of the roots, rocks and stems of our past, we are ready to work with sowing. Here we will discover that the seeds to be planted in our hearts are most magical seeds of infinite potential. We receive these from the Unseen—they are actually divine qualities that take root, mu-

[73] Hazrat Inayat Khan, *The Sufi Message of Hazrat Inayat Khan*, Vol. 1: The Way Of Illumination (Geneva: International Sufi Movement, 1960), p. 94.

tate and evolve in our being. This sowing, an evolution that takes place both inside and outside of us, can only begin through our willingness, our openness to receive.

The seeds sown in our being change the very template of the soul. They make it more possible for love, harmony and beauty to take precedence in our world. However unfathomable to our logic, these seeds can literally rewrite our past as they give shape to our future. This is possible because the world behind appearances is dynamic and creative, is truly a workable field. As we embrace and appreciate this field, this Emerald Earth, we are contributing something to its richness that will never be lost. In turn, the Earth responds by revealing its beauty and splendor to us.

The activity of sowing can be very challenging. Divine Mystery calls us right into the depths of life, and an intensified alchemy of our hearts removes any illusory separations between ordinary life and the sacred. Mystery is ever seeking expression, in order to be discovered and remembered, and we are integral to this creative activity. We, in turn, can only fully serve this evolutionary process to the degree that we willingly bring consciousness , freshness and ever new birth to our lives.

22
ON SOWING AND BEING SOWN

*The kingdom of heaven is likened
to a grain of mustard seed, which
a man took, and sowed in his
field, which indeed is the least of
all seeds, but when it is grown, it
is the greatest among herbs, and
becometh a tree, so that the birds
of the air come and lodge in the
branches thereof.*
          —*Matthew 13:31*

Planting seeds—Hawaiian dancers

OUR INDIVIDUAL BEINGS ARE AS LIVING SEED. We contain an infinite spark of Divine life, and have somehow been set into the ground of creation in order to bring forth a beautiful and fruitful plant.

To resolve any hesitation we might have about this situation, a certain shift in our understanding is necessary. Here again we invoke the poet Hafiz, who warns of the importance, after the long journey of coming here, of fully arriving at the port of our life.

Hafiz's warning is for all of us; coming close to the fulfillment of a long journey we must not stop, but rather be willing to risk everything. It is in this spirit that our focus of meditation practice shifts, becoming a "meditation in life" rather than one apart from it. By this turning, we will begin to see the working of Mystery all around us, an orchestration and unveiling within this life, seeking our attention and wishing to communicate with us most directly. And while this communication can take place everywhere, it is most clear within the ever-appearing beauty of the natural world.

All the great wisdom traditions of the world teach that the soul has been created for a destiny and purpose. Malidoma Somé tells how, in the tradition of the native people of West Africa, it is understood that each soul has received a unique gift from its Creator, to be utilized in the fulfillment of its life purpose. The individual soul, ignited by a spark of love, is brought here to inherit and care for the bounty of the earth, and to pass on this bounty to future generations.

One story told in the tradition of the Kabbalah relates that the "Boundless" had a dream of a beautiful earth, abundant not only with food, clothing and shelter but with precious gems and flowers, all to be appreciated and held sacred. In this story, the kindled human soul is shown not only a glimpse of this earth, but a foretaste of the unique contribution that this being will make to this life.

There are two monumental complications in this otherwise simple story. First, an immediate forgetting takes place: As an angel touches a finger to the lips—making the indentation or "bow "of the top lip— the memory of one's future contribution is lost. Second, perhaps to make life most interesting, free will reigns and allows for all possibilities. The whole of one's life, from birth onward, is for the purpose of remembering one's contribution and then finding ways to fulfill it.

Given these complications, it is not difficult to see why we may easily miss the opportunity of our journey to earth. Without wisdom, we easily forget our true responsibility to unfolding, becoming preoccupied with life's demands and concerns rather than fulfilling the purpose for which we are here.

This story emphasizes well the tremendous care we must take in gaining understanding of our experience. Through curiosity and diligence, we have the possibility of remembering, of reading "the signs on the horizon and inside of ourselves," and thereby gaining the fullest meaning of our spiritual and human experience. As we meditate, and as the correspondence of inner and outer life begins to reveal itself, we realize how the Unseen is continually sowing our being with seeds of new life, ultimately so that we may offer these to the world around us.

23

THE HIDDEN TREASURE

*I was a hidden treasure, I loved to
be known and I created the world.*[74]

WITHIN THESE PRECIOUS MO-
MENTS of earthly exis-
tence, we are called to
fulfill a purpose that is beyond our
personal evolution or our liberation
from illusions. The Hidden Treasure
of existence reveals itself in each of
our lives, where it is ever creative of
beauty and freshness.

In the creative act of love that brought this life into being, a frag-
mentation has occurred, necessary veils put into place so that the full
symphony of life, with its broad range of emotional tones and themes,
can manifest.

In a Sufi version of the creation story, Reality appeared as the
result of great longing, a "sigh" of Beauty and Compassion seeking to
be expressed. It was within a deep dream state that mystic Muhyiuddin
Ibn Arabi heard Divine Mystery exclaiming: "*I was a Hidden Treasure,
and I loved to be known.*" In a generous outpouring of love, creation appeared as the vehicle by which Reality could know itself, could manifest something of its beauty and profundity. Related stories say this
yearning arose because the Universe realized its own bounty but felt
a kind of "suffocation of its Names." The glorious richness and un-
bounded potentiality of Being wished to be manifest in this life.

The relief from a solitude of Unity, this passionate breath of
Love, has become our life. The longing we feel, and our frustration
when we cannot find or manifest beauty, are a reliving of an original
feeling of constriction within us. The Divine spark in our being wishes
to see and bring forth all that is beautiful, and this is why all our
habitual and uncreative reactions to life are so painful to us. And it is
for this reason too that our attainment of an interior meditative state is
not fully satisfactory to us. We know it is only a halfway point in our

---

[74] Muhyiuddin Ibn Arabi, *Wisdom of the Prophets* (Gloucestershire, England: Beshara
Publications, 1975), p. 8.

journey to awakening.

While the metaphysics can be daunting, we all sense within ourselves the longing that is described here. The Sufis call this longing *Ishq*, the spark of Universal Passion. It is this *Ishq* that becomes the drama of love, infinitely playful, sometimes excruciatingly painful and always bringing new life.

The science of chaos confirms something of the way that the "Hidden Treasure" seeks expression in our lives. In describing how, under proper conditions, chaos and turbulence produce new and more elegant structures, this science is simply describing Nature's preference for beauty. But while science cannot impute a motive to the universe, the wisdom traditions can. The mystic sees that the preference for beauty found in nature is a kind of coding by which the intelligence, elegance and underlying order of the universe reveal themselves.

Nature teaches that it is by experimentation and error that evolution proceeds. Mutations—sudden leaps in evolution—often come from some accident or break from the past that allows life to emerge in a new way. In our own life, taking new directions and making mistakes sometimes yield a richer understanding and a fulfillment that could not have otherwise come. Learning from our experience and becoming creative amidst the turbulence we face allow us to discover the pre-eternal "Hidden Treasure," coming to know its fulfillment in our lives. In the words of Inayat Khan, "Hail to my exile from the Garden of Eden to the earth! If I had not fallen, I should not have had the opportunity of probing the depths of life."[75]

[75] Hazrat Inayat Khan, *Complete Sayings, Gayan,* (New Lebanon, NY: Sufi Order Publications, 1978), p. 53.

24

THE YEAST OF A NEW CREATION

Creation... is the pre-eternal and continuous movement by which Being is manifest at every instant in a new cloak.[76]

ANCIENT LORE TELLS OF A CERTAIN LEAVEN—or "yeast"—preserved since the dawning of human life on the planet. The yeast was the remainder of the clay that was used to form the earthly bodies of Adam and Eve.[77] According to this lore, it is this life-bearing substance that we are called to rediscover through the spiritual journey, and by which a new creation—a new heaven and new earth–emerges.

Yeast is alive, and it truly is ancient, the substance of the earliest of life forms. In the story it represents the true spiritual knowledge that has been present and passed on from the time that human beings first inhabited the earth.

The "yeast" in our depths is a catalyst, a quickening energy and intelligence, our creative imagination brought to bear on dense matter. It is the realization that the sacred is present, that magic is present in every moment. The yeast is activated by the freshness and spontaneity of our being, coming forth from our depths and seeking its resonance and mirror in the sacred presence of life. In other words the creative imagination brings itself alive, brings out the active power of a ferment that meets and also transforms the world. In practical terms, when we meet life with freshness, it responds to us with the same—with surprise, with ease, sometimes with greater challenges, but always with new possibilities, new vistas. As Henry Corbin writes, the clay itself is to be found in a world where the "impossible becomes possible," an "Earth of Imagination" or, in our language, an Emerald Earth.

[76] Henry Corbin, *Alone with the Alone: Creative Imagination in the Sufism of Ibn Arabi* (Princeton: Bollingen Series XCI, Mythos edition, 1998), p. 200.

[77] Henry Corbin, *Spiritual Body and Celestial Earth* (Princeton: Bollingen Series, XCI:2, 1977), pp. 135-43.

As we have illustrated in the first part of this book, guidance tends to come first from outside, and most of us greatly benefit from the help of living and past teachers, the spiritual explorers who have received such guidance and acted upon it. Yet guidance from the outside can at best help us to reach our own inner spiritual guide, referred to by the Sufis as the "Khidr of the soul." Khidr, the "green man" we spoke of earlier, tells of his own function in our life:

> *I am transcendent reality, and I am the tenuous thread that brings it very close. I am the secret of the human being in the act of existing.... I am the invisible one who is the object of worship.... I am the guardian of the world of human nature.... I cause myself to be in every concept and to be manifested in every dwelling. I am the one who stands at the confluence of the two seas, the one who plunges into the river of the Where, the one who drinks from the source of the source. I am the guide of the fish in the sea of divinity.*[78]

Khidr is our guidance and also our creative power, a power that must be cultivated, affirmed, and, most importantly, utilized wisely in the service of life. The "Khidr of the soul" is attained by listening to the voice of the Earth telling us how we can be of service. In our listening we discover the same fecundity as Nature Herself, and the passion that brings a world of Creative Beauty into being. Here we realize that true passion is a receptive activity, an opening to the very power that creates and infuses life.

When we learn the subtle art of aligning the passion of our hearts with service to beauty, we bring forth an Emerald Earth. In this way, like the emerald, we reflect both an ancient light and the wisdom of the living Earth. The ancient living yeast within us, informed by our life, brings a new consciousness to moment-to-moment experience. Life becomes what it truly is—a new creation, a fresh and ever creative act.

[78] 'Abd al-Karim Jili "The Journey of the Stranger and the Conversation with Khizr," in Henry Corbin, *Spiritual Body and Celestial Earth* (Princeton: Bollingen Series, XCI, 1969), pp. 156-57.

PRACTICES—SOWING SEEDS OF AN EMERALD EARTH

The meditations in this section emphasize bringing creativity, intelligence and wisdom to bear on the challenges in the world around us. Each of the practices here is a creative act, by which we not only sow but mutate seeds, thoughts, passion and intentions within our being.

Practice #13: Walking Meditation—The Walk and Attunement of the Bodhisattva

We began exploring inner cultivation through practices of concentration and contemplation, balancing our tone and rhythm, and tuning our heart. The next aspect of meditation is the cultivation of receptivity to the seeds of inspiration and potential that stream into our beings and make our lives fruitful.

A simple and most powerful practice for this stage is a walking "meditation with open eyes." Certain traditions (such as Zen) include walking practice immediately after sitting in meditation. Practicing walking with meditative awareness helps us to keep an expanded attunement while transitioning into the movement and rhythm of everyday life.

> *There are many ways of walking. We often find that we are walking aimlessly, without attention to our feet, without attention to our breath, without awareness of the sacredness of life and of our essential nature. Try to walk with a deepened attention centered in the heart. Be aware of the rhythm of your breathing, aware of your interconnectedness with all beings, with all of life.*
>
> *To add a further dimension, concentrate on the bodhisattva, the human being who is approaching spiritual awakening and, instead of leaving the world behind, has taken a vow to help free others from suffering and bring compassion and mercy to the Earth.*
>
> *While bodhisattvas are usually associated with the Buddhist tradition, there are, in fact, many beings in other traditions who carry the same function of helping humanity. And since the bodhisattva is an embodiment of divine qualities, concentrating on one of these beings literally sows the seeds of the same divine quality within us. For example, concentrating on Bodhisattvas*

Chenrezig or Quan Yin, we begin to feel compassion and mercy; concentrating on the being of the prophet Abraham, we feel divine power and strength; concentrating on Mary, we become pure being and empty of self; focusing on St. Francis we feel the sacred unity of all of nature.

Try slowing your walk down to half its usual pace. You will find your breath slows down as well. In turn, slowing down our walking and breathing causes the mind to stop racing. Become more fully present with each step and breath. As you walk, let any heavy thoughts drain out through the feet into the ground.

Center your energy below the navel, feeling connected to a deeper reservoir of energy. Sink below the surface activity of the mind's endless chatter. Take each step as a fresh beginning.

Try walking as Quan Yin, feeling tremendous awareness, intention and purpose, wholly selfless. Place each foot down with the utmost care and heart-based compassion, walking gently upon the Earth, caring for all beings.

As Quan Yin walks, she takes the seeds of compassion, cupped in her left hand and held at the level of her heart, and with her right hand gently offers them, one seed at a time, onto the Earth. With the fingertips of the right hand, release the seed and allow the palm to open completely. With each step, sow seeds of compassion and mercy in a very simple and humble manner, with no rush, no grief or anxiety.

Walk with great care, feeling your feet to be rooted in the Earth. Once you have experienced the depth and consciousness of this walk you can leave out the outer gestures, bringing the attunement down into the heart, simply walking. You carry the feeling of the compassion directly through your glance, your breath, your heart and your rhythm. This attunement can be very healing not only to your own being but to the life around you. Problems and obstacles can subtly dissolve in the showering and sowing of compassion.

The further development of this practice, more suited to everyday life, is to walk at your normal pace. Practice walking with gratitude in the feet, compassion and love in the heart and truth in the shoulders, extending above the head. Don't allow yourself to be continually pulled by the circumstances around you. Watch your footsteps, and see where each step is taking you. From your open heart sow fresh seeds wherever you go. Contemplate these words:

> *The Sufi is one whose thought keeps pace with the foot, i.e., one is entirely present: one's soul is where one's body is, and one's body is where one's soul is, and one's soul where one's foot is, and one's foot where one's soul is. This is a sign of presence without absence.*[79]

Practice #14: Creative Imagination Practice

From more passive forms of meditation we move into the realm of active, creative meditation. Here we add vision and possibility to the acts of concentration and meditation. These relate to the process of sowing, and we add an important caution about the need for discrimination about the seeds we receive and sow.

We open to seeds of inspiration—of healing; of compassion; of beauty; of care for self, others and our Earth. These seeds, coming from the place of harmony and beauty in our being, are what we wish to encourage. Recognizing our true being, we see clearly how our striving to justify ourselves or to gather material possessions or power are misconstrued attempts to compensate for feelings of inadequacy or loss. Once we know which seeds to encourage, meditation and concentration practices provide ground, moisture, sun and air for growth and blossoming.

In this stage we are drawing upon the creative power within our being. The orientation reflects a subtle leap in consciousness and a turning point in spiritual practice. Here, while still aware of life's illusory aspect, we must give value to the world of separation we find ourselves in. We realize that if we want to help out we must invest our attention and learn to hold in consciousness two seemingly contradictory perspectives: unity and variety. In sacred traditions, there are different ways of referring to this challenge. The Tibetans speak of "becoming a child of illusion" in post-meditation practice. The Sufis say essentially the same thing in a teaching that "Reality demands a Veil," a paradox

---

[79] Hujwiri, *The Kashf Al-Mahjub of Al Hujwiri,* trans. R. Nicholson (London, Gibb Memorial Trust, 1976), p. 39.

to be explored further in Chapter 32, below.

To simultaneously give value to both Ultimate truth and the world around us, we might see creation as an artist's palette, and our lives as the brushes and colors on this palette. The artist moves the brush and uses the colors, and yet can only do so though our actions, our life. To add complexity to the image, the brush strokes and colors require our choices, and yet we never really know all the influences that may be at work. If, however, in the face of uncertainty we listen deeply and live openly and authentically, we will be able to tap into the continual creative process of Being.

We had a taste of a practice of creative imagination within the "Light Upon a Light" meditation above (Practice #12). The next practice asks us to strengthen and give unique expression to the qualities within us seeking to manifest. Emphasizing "meditation in life," this practice uses intention and creative vision to affect both our inner and outer worlds.

Focus on the seeds you want to sow in life, holding these with clear concentration. Hold your vision as the object of concentration before you, affirming it and improving upon it using the creative faculty of the mind. Take a pledge to practice until you are no longer pulled by all the other thoughts and circumstances that vie for your attention. Examine each day your ability to uphold this concentration, to stay with a creative "view" in the midst of life. Learn, in this practice, to concentrate without rigidity, with ease and with no judgment in the moments when your attention is diverted. Keep returning to the practice, trusting in your intention, in the alchemy taking place in your being, and in the effect of this practice on the life around you.

Practice #15: The Use of A Sacred Name or Phrase

The Lord's Name is the boat to cross over the world-ocean. Practice such a way of life.

—*Guru Granth Sahib*[80]

So remember Me, and I shall remember you.

—*Qur'an Sura 2, Verse 152*

In every great spiritual tradition, some invocation of a sacred

---

[80] *Guru Granth Sahib*, Vol. II, ed. Pritam Singh Chahil (New Delhi, 1990), p. 535.

word, divine name or phrase is used. The practitioners of mystical Christianity, Islam and Judaism, as well as Buddhist, Hindu and Sikh sages, have sophisticated sciences based on the visualization of and repetition of these *mantras.* The names and phrases that are used have been passed down from the great teachers who first used them. It is understood that the words themselves carry a powerful blessing and transformative energy.

The simplest form of this practice is the centering of a sacred name or phrase in a chakra or energy center, most often the heart. With the help of the breath, the sacred word is "placed" mentally in the heart, or, for some practices, in the third eye (in the center of the forehead) or in the crown center, above the head. For example, the desert hermits use the phrase *Kyrie eleison* (literally meaning *Lord have mercy*), and their Sufi counterparts use a name of God. The particular techniques vary: one might breathe a phrase or word into the heart on the inhalation and the same or another name or phrase out on the exhalation. The practice usually begins aloud, softly at first, then dropping to a whisper, ending as thought held in the heart.

Researcher Gray Henry notes that the word *eleison* shares the same root as the Greek word for the olive tree and its oil—most powerful symbols in the spiritual traditions of the Near East. An olive twig was brought to Noah as a healing mercy, symbolic of a crucial divine message that "we should be able to live and become all that we are called to be." To the Sufis, invoking a mystical interpretation of a Qur'anic verse, the oil from an olive tree guides and illuminates the soul, and ultimately brings the soul to the realization of all of life—and particularly the life of the human being—to be the manifestation of a "Light upon a Light."[81]

These allusions are most relevant to this practice. When the repetition of a sacred name is used deeply and sincerely, it literally brings light into our being, clearing away the rust from the heart that prevents us from realizing ourselves and our lives as "light upon a light." Our intuition deepens tremendously and, with practice, objects of nature and life situations speak most directly to us.

The profound effect of the repetition of the sacred name is secretly alluded to in myths and fairy tales. It is the *"Open Sesame,"* the rub-

---

[81] See "St. Seraphim of Sarov in Sufi Perspective," by Gray Henry, in *Paths of the Heart, Sufism and the Christian East,* ed. James Cutsinger (Bloomington, IN: World Wisdom Publications), pp. 24-31.

bing of Aladdin's lamp, bringing help and guidance. The sacred word opens the door of the heart, purifying and clearing foreign elements and impressions, giving new vision and insight. Most importantly, repetition of a sacred word brings the heart fully alive, which is crucial to our freedom and happiness. Inayat Khan stressed that it is only when our consciousness is in the heart that we can be free and be whole:

> *Heart not only heals mind, heart heals itself. Through the bloodstream heart heals the body, and to a certain extent helps the mind, but through breath, will and the inner light, heart can completely purge the mind of all its pain.*

The chanting of sacred names is often used in a yoga or meditation group. It brings a deep and powerful sense of devotion and, for some at least, an ecstatic communion with the Divine. Other than such a use, the practice of the "prayer of the heart" should be undertaken with the help of an experienced guide. There is a whole science of individual spiritual guidance using sacred sounds and Divine names, and there are guides from many traditions who have the insight necessary to make use of this science. Ideally, such a guide should be directly linked with a sacred tradition, be deeply experienced with spiritual practice and be someone with whom the student feels a strong resonance and trust. In most of the spiritual traditions, such guides do not ask for any kind of recompense for their guidance.

Practice #16: The Journey of Love[82]

The hidden desire of the creator is the secret of the whole creation.[83]

In this meditation we reflect upon the Soul's journey from abstraction, from unity into this life on earth. Pure Love, pure Desire, is the power that has kindled this world, that moves the planets and galaxies. It is absolutely cosmic, and yet it seeks expression in the minutest details and experiences of our lives, breath by breath. For this reason, the fact that our passion and love are alive and burning is crucial not only to our mediations but to the effectiveness and impact of our service to life.

Here we will be exploring the way that desire becomes a key to recognizing our own divine essence. First, we acknowledge that desire is close to our core, to our natural state. In other words, we can translate the

---

[82] This is a meditation based on teachings by Pir Zia Inayat Khan, 2006.

[83] Hazrat Inayat Khan, *Complete Sayings, Gayan* (New Lebanon, NY: Sufi Order Publications, 1978), p. 330.

truth that the universe is continually appearing anew, in every moment, into a concrete awareness of our own desire nature, and the continual arising of desire within us. For many spiritually oriented people, this truth can be difficult to accept. And yet, when understood properly, it can help us to be most fully alive and fruitful to the life around us, becoming infinitely compassionate rather than infinitely selfish.

In the Sufi tradition, the embrace of desire is evident in the very name that is given to the student disciple. The student is the *mureed* which means the "desiring one." As Sufi teacher Zia Inayat Khan explains, the word *mureed* is traditionally recognized as a Divine name, i.e., it is a name used to identify an attribute of the Divine in manifestation. This means that when we are in an authentic state of desiring, we are manifesting something of our divinity.

Of course there are problems and complications when we embrace desire. Desire is unlimited, and seeking the fulfillment of our every object of desire is not the point: this would overload us with responsibilities, make our lives too complicated, and never really give us satisfaction.

When we are unaware of our deepest desires, our apparent objects of desire are simply masks, mere substitutes for reality. On the other hand, approaching desire with wisdom and awareness, it becomes a compass pointing to our deepest identity. Then, in touch with our depths, we can best understand and fulfill the deepest desires of the soul.

There is a very practical means for using desire as such a compass for getting in touch with our own depths. An instruction given within a mystical tantric teaching is most helpful: when desire arises, the student is taught to see beyond the particular object of desire to the deep impulse that is behind the desire. The deep impulse is understood to be divine in nature, very powerful and life affirming. In formal language, the practice is described as follows:

> *When a desire appears, the aspirant should, with the mind withdrawn from all objects, fix her or his mind on it as the very Self, then he or she will have the realization of the Essential Reality.* [84]

In essence, all of life is the impulse of *Ishq*, of pure Love seeking expression. Love seeks its mirror in the beauty and satisfaction of this life. Here we offer some systematic contemplations for exploring more deeply into this mystery:

1. First, reflect deeply on a desire—on any desire—that is arising.

[84] From the *Sri Vijnana Bhairava Tantra*, an ancient Kashmiri text.

Feel its depths, beyond the object in which it is manifesting. Connect with its depths as pure Love, as Ishq. Reflect on the truth that we came from this energy, that it was this force which brought us into this life.

2. Go deeper, reflecting on a welling of deeper passion—the desire to bring into being the bounties of the Unseen. Recognize your passion as the longing to manifest a splendor beyond words, to give it form and substance, to give it expression. What is abstract wishes to become music, color, fragrance, swaying trees, exquisitely shaped flowers and shafts of light.

3. Even when absorbed in family and job responsibilities or other seeming "distractions," Love is continually calling us to manifest our deepest desires. Following guidance, we learn to live on a threshold between the world of Love and our everyday experience. From here we realize that our life is a continual opportunity and challenge to affirm love and beauty in this world.

4. Reflect on the way life has emerged from silence and emptiness, and then gradually evolved into more expressive forms— from rock to plant to insect and animal, to human. Reflect on the richness that is emerging in the evolution of our being. It is an ascent, filled with passion, creativity and ecstasy, and its emerald hue reflects the wisdom of our experience of the world of matter.

5. Focus on the heart, and realize it to be an infinite ocean of love, uniting and embracing all. Feel the heart awakening as a blossoming flower, emerging out of a black and fertile field of our life experience. Sense how this dark and fertile field holds everything, and does not reject anything—beauty and exaltation, pain, sacredness and struggle.

6. Each moment of our life is eternalized, essentialized within the cultivated heart. Allow yourself, in this practice, to become intoxicated with Love, embracing the mystery of Love that brought you here, and that now envelops you with compassion and connects you to the condition of splendor. In your creative imagination, let this splendor infuse the life around you with a green-gold color, and then an emerald color.

PART V: The Harvest—Realizing an Emerald Earth

Part V, The Harvest, describes the fulfillment of life. Here we explore the culmination of the whole process of creation, in which the Universe comes to know itself as nature and as humanity.

Introduction—A World Alive with Meaning

Why have I two eyes if not to behold Thy glorious vision?
Why have I two ears if not to hear Thy gentle whisper?
Why have I the sense of smell if not to breathe the essence of Thy spirit?
Why have I two lips, Beloved, if not to kiss Thy beautiful countenance?
Why have I two hands if not to work in Thy divine cause?
Why have I two legs if not to walk in Thy spiritual path?
Why have I a voice if not to sing Thy celestial song?
Why have I a heart, Beloved, if not to make it Thy sacred dwelling?[85]

THERE IS A BUDDHIST CELEBRATION CALLED "PLOWING DAY," celebrating the day of Buddha's first moment of awakening. Buddha's first opening came when he was a child sitting in the fields, watching the act of plowing. Buddha later described plowing—the turning of the soil and clearing the field of rocks and weeds—as symbolic of our inner life. He taught that the clearing of "the weeds of illusion" was the cure for suffering, revealing our deepest nature and opening the way to a fruit-bearing existence.

As we have stressed, the key to the harvest is becoming free from limited viewpoints and assessments. As Moses learned from his perplexing guide Khidr, and as Marpa taught by continually tearing down the houses that Milarepa built, we have to continually clear the field of our being, "beginning again," allowing our concepts and ideals to be set aside so that we can open to something more reliable, the magic of "reality" that comes through in each moment. The recognition of this miraculous reality is the fulfillment of our human journey.

Being awake is equivalent to what the Zen tradition calls *soshin* or "beginner's mind." Free of the weeds and stones of confused and hardened ways of being and thinking, the mind is transparent, fresh and fertile. In the words of Zen Master Shunryu Suzuki, "in the beginner's mind there are many possibilities, in the expert's mind, few."[86] To the

[85] Hazrat Inayat Khan, *Complete Sayings, Vadan* (New Lebanon, NY: Sufi Order Publications, 1978) p. 105.

[86] Shunryu Suzuki, *Zen Mind, Beginner's Mind* (New York: Weatherhill, 1997), p. 21.

beginner's mind, each seemingly ordinary moment is fresh and surprising, not limited by our habitual thinking or expectations, a miraculous event.

The harvest takes place in the clear light and crisp colors of autumn. And while we may only occasionally glimpse the fruits of our own lives, there are moments when the fullness of beauty shines through. The heavy stone of our limited, judgmental thinking is pushed aside so that our true being and true perception may rise again to life.

Opening ourselves to life's continual alchemy, we are transformed through patience and compassion, through realizing that life is ever-seeking opportunities to unfold through us. Even little pin pricks within our everyday experience play a crucial role in opening us, in making our hearts pure and fertile, and in bringing us to deep intimacy and communion with the Unseen.

We ourselves become gardeners of inner and outer life, working towards a harvest for all humanity. With fresh vision, we see that a new world is unfolding each moment, a "new creation in every breath," filled with beauty, freshness and possibility.

In the chapters that follow, we will explore this unique awakening and see how from it each of us is guided towards greater service to life. If we are to live by this guidance, we must confront some essential questions. Can we look beyond our ordinary reactions, beyond blame, beyond rejection of any aspect of our experience, and align ourselves with the freshness and evolutionary thrust of life? Can we seek a sacred relationship with the manifest world, seeing that the elements are the servants of Divine Art, as sacred substance, emotion, passion, light and intelligence? Can we devote ourselves to finding ways we might better serve our families, our communities and the natural world? The answers to these questions will have tremendous implications for our lives and the lives of those who come after us.

25
THE GREAT WORK

When the body is redeemed in the holy mystery of participation in an animate and theophanic cosmos, hope will again arise for the future of our green globe, and what is more, true presence in the moment.[87]

I N THE STAGE OF THE HAR-
VEST, WE GAIN AN INTIMACY
with Divine guidance and
mystery. We realize tangibly that this entire world is a
spreading green prayer car-
pet, is the Emerald Tablet that
we can read and by which we are guided. We have a miraculous opportunity, through our gratitude and awe for life's mystery, and through
our relationship with the Earth, to bring divine awareness into its fullest expression in our world. As we discover the Divine in ourselves,
we realize that everything in creation—the plants, trees, insects and
animals, attests to the glory and beauty of an Unseen yet intimate mystery.

While life manifests divine beauty, our sacred Earth is suffering from terrible neglect and misuse. To truly express our gratitude for
this life we are called to take responsibility; we must truly "inherit the
Earth" and protect the natural world.

The work at the stage of the harvest is both inside and outside of
us, a work to protect this precious life and to sow the future garden of
the Earth. It is a task we must undertake each day, in each experience,
even when we do not have the slightest inkling of how to proceed. In
our unknowing, this responsibility calls us to be continually aware of
what life is asking of us.

In the remainder of this book, we emphasize awareness of the
link between inner and outer "work," inner and outer realities. The

---

[87] Pir Zia Inayat Khan, *The Holy Mysteries of the Elements* (New Lebanon, NY: Sufi
Order Publications, 2005), p. 10.

degradation of our environment is a mirror of problems in our own inner ecology and misconstrued values. To contribute positively to the outer environment we must confront, each day and each moment, the field of our minds and hearts. Through the clarity that emerges from this confrontation, we know ourselves to be truly united to the planet and to nature. Understood this way, the polluting of our earth, water and air is the poisoning of our body and energy field. When we gain intimacy with our own depths, we come to know that the Mystery behind this life is alive and communicative, and continually planting seeds of inspiration in us. Through the cultivation of our minds and hearts, we gain a receptivity and a capacity to cultivate seeds of fresh inspiration and potential. Only if we are creative and responsive, living in intimacy with the mystery that is far beyond our understanding, can our lives truly flourish.

In deep connection with ourselves we cannot help but be deeply connected with the Earth. We learn to listen to this Being's guidance and Her cry, and learn to act in ways that bring forth Her beauty.

Our intimacy with the Earth becomes an I-Thou rather than an I-It relationship. The Earth is not for our manipulation, but a living being whom we can love in a dynamic and caring relationship. As understood by the indigenous people of the world, the Earth is the Great Mother. In the ancient Zoroastrian tradition, She is recognized as the feminine archangel Spenta Armaiti, and care for Her is the most essential act of devotion. The Greek philosophers and also the Orthodox Christian tradition describe Sophia as the divine embodied in all of creation, who guides and reveals the deep wisdom of the Earth.

Recently, the seventeenth Karmapa Ogyen Trinley Dorje, the head of the Kagyu Lineage of Tibetan Buddhism (see Chapter 3) expressed his concern for our natural world, and for the dangerous situation in which we find ourselves. In his words:

> We should consider the possibility that exactly the harm we cause to another comes directly to us.... I personally feel that now is an important time to warmly embrace the environment.... There are very clear signs and indications that our environment is aching.... is suffering— there are symptoms and expressions. Everything that is occurring in terms of harm and destruction of the environment, degradation of the environment... this is not taking place because there is no choice, or because we are totally helpless. That is not so.... It is apparent that those

*of us who get the best use of the environment, abuse it the most. So now
there are all the signs of the degradation, the suffering and agony of the
world we live in. We might need to reconsider and embrace our world
with some loving care.*"[88]

This is the "Great Work" we are called to—no longer an individual journey to enlightenment—but now a collective work of caring
for each other and our natural world. Though this Great Work begins
inside of us, it will only be completed in an uplifted world and in the
restoration and preservation of our soil, water, air and ecological balance.

Of course our evolving understanding of this Great Work is
nothing new to the wisdom keepers among the indigenous peoples of
the world. These guides have taught for thousands of years that we
need to revere and treasure the elements, and the gift of life these offer.
Earth, water, fire, air and ether serve the harmony and beauty of life,
bringing renewal by their dynamism and powers of purification. When
we too respect and seek to serve the same harmony and beauty of life,
we align and in turn are helped by the same elements.

The natural reverence and sacred relationship we need to cultivate is well reflected in this song of the seventeenth Karmapa:

Ah, World! It's on your lap do we live and die,
It's on you we play out all our pleasures and pains.
You are such a very old home of ours.
We treasure and hold you dear forever.
We wish to transform you into the pure realm of our dreams.
Into an unprejudiced land where all creatures are equal.
We wish to transform you into a loving warm gentle goddess.
We wish so very firmly to embrace you.
To that end be the ground which sustains us all.
Do not show us the storms of your nature's dark side.
And we too will transform you, all your corners
Into fertile fields of peace and happiness.
May the harvest of joyfulness and freedom's million sweet
Scents fulfill our limitless infinite wishes, so we pray.[89]

[88] Seventeenth Gyalwa Karmapa, *Under the Bodhi Tree, The Jewel Ornament of
Liberation,* video by Mark Eliot and Lama Karma Chodrak, 2003 Monlam Festival.

[89] Seventeenth Gyalwa Karmapa, composed for the Monlam Prayer Festival, Bodhgaya,
India, 2005.

26
THE CHILD OF THE MOMENT

Every instant we are dying and returning.... Every moment the world is renewed, but we are unaware because it still looks the same.... Life is ever new, like a fresh stream.... From its swiftness it appears continuous, like a firebrand whirling rapidly in your hand.[90]

The instant of time is a sharp sword that cuts the root of the future and the past and obliterates care of yesterday and tomorrow from the heart.[91]

Beginner's Mind, based on the calligraphy of Shunryu Suzuki

Every moment the universe emerges anew. However stable our accustomed physical reality may appear, the universe is pulsing, changing, contracting and expanding, continually dying and being reborn.

The ever-arising moment is free from the conditioning of the past and the apprehension of the future. It is by virtue of this truth that the spiritual disciple can be continually renewed, freed from the prisons of regret, blame and apprehension.

Buddhist teacher Chogyam Trungpa emphasized that we miss the true magic of the present because we are continually experiencing life out of our memories. We dwell on the past and our hopes for the future, missing the point and the preciousness of this moment.

Meditating with eyes open in everyday life, we can make it an ongoing practice to be renewed with each breath. Facing all the stresses around us, we can open to the perspectives that spiritual explorers of the past only attained in solitude. Aware of the freshness of each instant, we can leave behind our habitual and reactive states of mind.

The initial step in fully coming into the present is in remembering that we are taking part in a well-orchestrated and universal dream. Most mysteriously, this dream is asking us to work within it, to bring

---

[90] Jelaluddin Rumi, The *Mathnawi*, R. Nicholson, trans. (Cambridge, England: Gibb Memorial Trust, 1926), authors' renditions of verses 1140-44

[91] Hujwiri, *Kashf Al-Mahjub of Al Hujwiri*, R. Nicholson, trans. (London: Gibb Memorial Trust), rendition of pp. 367-68 by Pir Vilayat Khan.

the realization and clarity of our being to bear upon everyday situations. Knowing this great secret fills our life with opportunities to recognize beauty, abundance and mercy, and to be ever present.

The "dream" of this life is not merely a phantasm, a creation of our personal ego. It is a much grander dream, a play of Universal Creativity. The Mystery of Being experiences this dream through our journey through life. The Source and Goal of all experiences life through our experience. Within the ever-unfolding creativity of our experience, the Universe seeks to bring forth new worlds of beauty and love.

It is our challenge to realize ourselves as having a vital role within this universal dream. When we learn to fully receive each instant, our vision opens to life's well-orchestrated play. Each moment, we realize, is *the* crucial instant, a time to relish, to remember our Source, to be grateful for all the chaos and peace, joy and strife, tenderness and difficulty of being, in Rumi's words, the "lovely vitality of a human being."

Ultimately, awakening calls us to become a child of each moment, listening and seeing deeply. It is from this freshness that we realize each instant as a living and sacred scripture, ever revealing itself, ever seeking to communicate all the richness and possibility of Being. The same is true for each of us: In each instant we are a fresh departure from who we were the moment before, and we need not be imprisoned by our self-image, past impressions or even by the ancestral memories carried in our blood.

Our awareness of the existence of an ever-new creation allows us to fully honor each moment. By a childlike appreciation and unknowing in the face of a great mystery, we realize ourselves as Universal Being, born anew in each miraculous instant.

27

AWAKENING IN LIFE

Love is begging us
to awaken.
Pleading, calling, urging.
This is why the holy books
sound so weighty.
A call of a parent afraid
for her child,
a lover longing for the
Beloved, now.
The Friend does not want
us to miss the awesome
beauty of our life,
to miss the chance to die
before we die, to become
who we truly are.
To be happiness, joy, light
and praise.
Come, the beloved says, let
us give up being so
predictable, with all the
familiar routines that make us dull.
Leap into the dance, listening every moment for the voice
that melts your heart, that asks you to accept pain,
to forgive, forge, open.
To love, to love, and to love.
It is time, and there is no other time.
Resurrection is today.
Every objection, every concept and hesitation,
every desperate calling wound,
can melt away, and reveal an open door.
It is time, in this amazing and improbable moment,
to remember, to live and to bow in gratitude to Mystery.[92]

Pilgrims at the Golden Temple,
Amritsar, India

S PIRITUAL AWAKENING ASKS US TO MEET LIFE DIFFERENTLY, and in so doing to bring our deepest wisdom and potential to bear on the world around us. Our talent and creativity come to life instantaneously when we affirm the sacred in everything we do.

[92] Poem by the authors

Energy and intelligence arise when needed, especially as we cultivate our being, plowing and clearing obstacles that would hinder us, and realizing the ways that we can be of service to life.

Our life struggles and seeming shortcomings become the raw material of the cultivation of our hearts and minds. Understood rightly, what we may view as negative aspects of our being provide energy and substance that, when transformed, become positive forces. Here the story a Tibetan spiritual guide, Yeshe Tsogyel, will help us.

Yeshe Tsogyel was the closest disciple of the esteemed eighth-century teacher Padmasambhava, who brought Buddhism to Tibet. Sometimes referred to as "Lady Tsogyel," this revered teacher apparently underwent most extreme hardships in her spiritual journey. Ultimately she became the source of some of the richest teachings of tantric Buddhism within the land of Tibet.

During a journey,[93] Yeshe Tsogyel was confronted by dangerous thieves. As the thieves surrounded her, Tsogyel's first response was to sing. The melody of her song was so profound that the thieves all went into a state of deep meditation. Their aggression and maliciousness turned into serenity and curiosity. Instead of robbing her they asked her to sing another song to them.

Yeshe Tsogyel proceeded to offer a teaching to the thieves. She instructed them to recognize that every negative emotion could be transformed into a powerful force of enlightenment. Anger, pride, insatiable desire, jealousy and ignorance, when recognized and transformed, would become wisdom and qualities of enlightened body, speech and mind.

Yeshe Tsogyel taught the thieves that aggression and malice were actually distorted expressions of the radiance and clarity of the mind. Her insight here reflects the Buddhist teaching that, in digging below the surface we find the "mirror-like" wisdom of our being. As aggression and malice are transformed, this wisdom emerges as a joy of freedom from appearances. In the clarity that ensues we recognize that bliss fills our universe, permeating form. We recognize, in the light of this clarity, the possibilities for beauty in situations which would ordinarily be seen as problematic. The ultimate antidote for the poison of aggression is the clarity that altogether uproots the idea of an "other" that one might blame.

The second negative condition that Yeshe Tsogyel taught about was being dominated by pride and complacency. These cover over a

---

[93] This story is found in *Sky Dancer: The Life and Songs of the Lady Yeshe Tsogyel,* by Keith Dowman (Ithaca, NY: Snow Lion Publications, 1996), pp. 44-47.

"wisdom of equality," a recognition of equality and solidarity with all beings, all conditions and all worlds. The antidote for pride and complacency is not to try to dissolve them, but rather to affirm the nobility of others, ultimately of all beings. The "pride" then becomes impersonal a sense of respect and gratitude for the precious jewel of this creation.

The third condition that Yeshe Tsogyel addressed was incessant desire, the hungering for things and for experience. In a way parallel to the Sufi perspective on desire, she described personal desire as a reflection of the desire that fuels all of creation, rather than something that could be eliminated. Transforming desire is practiced by paying attention to and harnessing the raw energy behind desire, rather than always needing to obtain and possess an object of desire. This transformed response is akin, in Buddhist terms, to a "discriminating wisdom" that deeply values and is contented with life, a very beneficial attitude that can bring forth great generosity.

The negative reactions of envy, alienation and jealousy were the fourth subject of Yeshe Tsogyel's teachings. These she explained as the distorted expressions of unimpededness, efficiency and success, called in the Buddhist tradition "all-accomplishing wisdom." Exploring below the surface of the jealous, judging and resentful aspects of mind, we find that there are impressions of doubt and failure. Digging deeper, we find a natural capacity for accomplishment, completion, and success. And while this capacity is limited and imprisoning when oriented towards us alone, it is especially powerful and expansive when devoted to the well-being of all.

Addressing a final trait, Yeshe Tsogyel showed the thieves that ignorance and stupidity are distorted expressions of a deep experience of spaciousness. These are, when transformed, the expressions of a vast "wisdom of universal spirit." When such wisdom is encountered by our limited human consciousness, it brings awe and humility, a deep state of unknowing. This unknowing, in turn, can be what brings the awakening soul to the spiritual path. It allows us to open to guidance, to turn and hold fast to a path, to seek refuge and relief from the dreamlike nature of our experience. Looking beyond our ignorance, we can see what Yeshe Tsogyel called a "visionary panorama," illumined by wisdom. Beholding this panorama, we realize how even our most uninformed states are imbued with guidance and light, opening us to spaciousness and wisdom.

Though set in a distant land and time, the story of Lady Yeshe Tsogyel is most relevant to our everyday world. Acknowledging and embracing the seemingly negative aspects of our mind and psyche, it teaches about the power of transformation: within each of us is the power to transform aggression, pride, insatiable desire, jealousy and ignorance. The fruits of this transformation are bliss and possibility, a pride in the dignity of creation, discernment and choice that bring us to a more beautiful and meaningful world.

Seeing the way our seeming afflictions rob us of our natural freedom and freshness can give rise to a powerful aspiration within us for enlightened states of consciousness. If we can learn to recognize but not act out of our negative states, instead mining the gems that are buried beneath a surface affliction, we can bring a profound gift into our life. Facing pain, plowing deeply enough to bring anger, pride, inordinate desire, envy, and ignorance to the surface for clearing, we have the opportunity of removing ourselves from the fortress of protection that our ego has created. Having the courage to continually "tear down the house" of the ego's resistance and inertia brings us to the true life we are here to live.

The essence of Yeshe Tsogyel's teaching is the realization that all is a mirror, that negative emotions, judgment or criticism come from a failure to recognize the treasures hidden in our being. Finding acceptance, forgiveness and compassion for ourselves and others allows us to transform our seemingly negative states and to discover and mine the priceless gems buried within us. When this happens, our understanding and perception open most fully. We see that every challenging circumstance brings new energy and a greater awareness of the sacred presence that embraces all of existence.

28
THE PURPOSE OF LIFE

Every soul has a definite task, and the fulfillment of each individual purpose can alone lead the soul; illumination comes through the medium of the soul's own talent.[94]

WHILE A DAILY MEDITATION PRACTICE IS CRUCIAL, the "harvest" of spiritual unfolding calls us to learn how to meditate with eyes open in the middle of everyday life. As found in the story of Yeshe Tsogyel, true meditation teaches us to use obstacles and difficulties to muster energy and potential and to enrich our lives. Meditation helps us to realize that we are truly asleep—that life events and circumstances are a dream before the soul, yet a dream that can be properly interpreted, understood and changed.

Our life is a living scripture, rich with symbols that inspire us and help us remember our true being. Just as we are challenged during periods of meditation to use patience and diligence and to work through limitations and resistance, so we are called to a very similar kind of "work" in our everyday lives. As difficult circumstances appear, we have the opportunity to bring the fruits of meditation to bear on all aspects of our lives, and to thereby enrich the world around us with clarity and harmony.

The Persian poet Saadi once wrote, "Every soul is born for a certain purpose, and the light of that purpose is kindled in the soul." Pir Vilayat Khan emphasized how this purpose is elegantly linked to the rest of life, explaining that "when you find your piece within the puzzle of life, everyone else does too." This is the crucial link, the play of the individual within the universal.

Our "piece in the puzzle," our unique purpose, is not fixed. Rather, there is always some note that we are called to strike, and this can manifest in varying ways in different circumstances and stages of our lives. At the same time, this note is linked to our unique talents and

[94] Hazrat Inayat Khan, *Complete Sayings, The Bowl of Saki* (New Lebanon, NY: Sufi Order Publications, 1978), p. 246.

skills, a unique expression of the intelligence, generosity and creativity of the universe that we have the privilege to contribute to life.

Because our interests, talents and desires point towards our unique contribution, honoring and nurturing these is crucial to unfolding our sense of purpose, our enthusiasm and our joy of living. While this may not sound like a "spiritual orientation," it is the key to a natural spirituality, a state of happiness and satisfaction, inside and out. Connection with our unique expression of being, our deepest passion, is also the expression of the Divine desire to manifest beauty in this life, to join heaven and earth. By honoring and cultivating our deepest passion we naturally contribute to the beauty and satisfaction of all of the life around us.

Honoring our depths often runs counter to conventional values and the expectations of those around us. Our life purpose reflects the evolutionary dynamics of life, which are elegant and yet most often do not conform to our plans and logic. The dynamic nature of an unfolding life purpose—and the unpredictable and yet elegant way it might play out—is well depicted in the classic Indian story of the great thief Shivaji. The story, amusing and yet factual, is retold by Sufi master Hazrat Inayat Khan:

> In the East there are various stories told about sages and saints who have awakened someone to the purpose of his particular life; and the moment that person was awakened his whole life changed. There is an account in the history of India of the life of Shivaji. There was a young robber who used to attack travelers passing along the way where he lived and he stole from them whatever he could. And one day before going to his work he came to a sage and greeted him and said, "Sage, I want your blessing, your help in my occupation." The sage asked what his occupation was. He said, "I am an unimportant robber." The sage said, "Yes, you have my blessing." The robber was very pleased, and went away and had greater success than before. Happy with his success he returned to the sage and greeted him by touching his feet and said, "What a wonderful blessing it is to be so successful." But the sage said, "I am not yet satisfied with your success, I want you to be more successful. Find three or four more robbers and join together and then go on with your work."
>
> Shivaji joined with four or five other robbers who went with him and again had great success. Once more he came to the sage and said, "I want your blessing." The sage said, "You have it. But still I am not

satisfied. Four robbers are very few. You ought to form a gang of twenty." So he found twenty robbers. And eventually there were hundreds of them.

Then the sage said, "I am not satisfied with the little work you do. You are a small army of young men, you ought to do something great. Why not attack the Mogul strongholds and push them out, so that in this country we may reign ourselves?" And so he did, and a kingdom was established. The sage could have said, "What a bad thing, what a wicked thing you are doing. Go in the factory and work!"

But the sage saw what Shivaji was capable of. Robbery was his first lesson, his "a-b-c." He had only a few steps to advance to be the defender of his country, and the sage realized that he was going to be a king, to release his people from the Moguls. The robbers did not see it, the young man did not think about it. He was pushed into it by the sage. The sage was not pushing him into robbery; he was preparing him for a great work.[95]

The story of Shivaji, a great hero in India's history, expresses something of the magnificent choreography that connects individual purpose with the universal. Since we do not have the luxury of a sage to advise us on our actions, we must for ourselves use conscience and deep probing to know when we are tapping into our true purpose. As with Shivaji, when we find and trust in our purpose we do find that it dovetails, often in surprising ways, with the life around us. We also come to sense that this note is most uniquely ours and that it is absolutely vital for our fulfillment:

Our happiness depends on striking that note; and the realization of that purpose is in the book of our heart. Open that book and look at it. All meditation and contemplation is only to open this book, to focus our mind, and to see what purpose there is in our life. And no sooner do we see that our ultimate goal and our life's object and happiness, our true health and well-being and our real wealth and welfare, are in the fulfillment of our purpose, than the whole trend of life will change.[96]

[95] Hazrat Inayat Khan, *The Sufi Message of Hazrat Inayat Khan.* Vol. VI: The Alchemy of Happiness (Delhi: International Sufi Movement, 1989), p. 35.

[96] Hazrat Inayat Khan, *The Sufi Message of Hazrat Inayat Khan*, Vol. X: Sufi Mysticism (Geneva: International Sufi Movement, 1979), p. 146-47.

29
THE MUSIC OF LIFE

Life to a wise person is music; and in that symphony he has to play a certain part. If one were feeling so low that one's heart was sounding a lower pitch, and the demand of life at that moment was that one should voice a higher pitch, then one would feel that one had failed in that music in which one was meant to play one's part fittingly. This is the test by which you can distinguish the old soul and the child soul. The child soul will give way to every feeling; the old soul will strike the higher note in spite of every difficulty. [97]

LIKE AN INTRICATE MUSICAL COMPOSITION, our life has an overall theme and purposefulness and yet also includes experimentation, counterpoint and seeming randomness.

Great pioneers of mathematics and science, such as Pythagoras and Kepler, saw that physical matter expresses musical harmony. While their elaborate theories may have seen more musical order in the "symphony of the spheres" than actually exists, there is a music within all of life that has been recognized by spiritual adepts of every age. Musical harmony is always seeking expression in our lives, and each of us has a crucial role in this symphony. In the words of Hazrat Inayat Khan:

In order to live in the world one should become a musician of life. Every person therein is a note, and the one who feels this way has an instrument before him: the whole world is an instrument upon which a symphony is to be played. [98]

[97] Hazrat Inayat Khan, *The Sufi Message of Hazrat Inayat Khan*, Vol. III: The Art of Personality (Geneva: International Sufi Movement, 1960), p. 198.

[98] Hazrat Inayat Khan, *The Sufi Message of Hazrat Inayat Khan*, Vol. XIV: Sufi Teachings, (Geneva: International Sufi Movement, 1963), p. 104.

The music of life is not metaphor but a clear expression of Reality. With insight and the wisdom of experience, we see how each moment offers us a choice: to strike a note that is most resonant and harmonious or one that is not. The harmonious note rings with possibility and is filled with energy, generosity and hope. The inharmonious note expresses resistance, our fears and suspicions, our weariness or inability to see a bigger picture.

Until we cultivate a deeper perspective, striking a higher note when we are not feeling well, when feeling attacked or when we are in a state of grief or sorrow can seem like a betrayal of our authenticity. But with wisdom we come to realize that our "true" note is the less reactive and more expansive one, whether or not we feel this to be so in a certain moment. The inharmonious note, however justified it may seem, is absolutely futile, and comes at the cost of our peace of mind. We know that a single moment of forgetfulness, in which we express rage or anger, can disturb us and the world around us very deeply. So, when situations seem to almost demand us to be reactive, a wise tact is to simply be patient with things as they are, recognizing the pain or constriction we are feeling to be as passing clouds. Learning, with practice, to surrender our seeming justification to react—and embracing with patience a momentary discomfort—will open us to tremendous freedom and creativity.

With this said, it is sometimes a very great challenge to not react and to instead strike a harmonious note. As we open our hearts and allow ourselves to be fully vulnerable, the challenge becomes even greater. Reactions seem to come more quickly, and we can be surprised to find that some inner "plowing" has uncovered a whole spectrum of negative tendencies and thought patterns that we were not aware of. To complicate the situation even more, with more sensitivity we more easily pick up anger, doubt and fear from others. Yet, despite these challenges, we can learn to not only check our reactions but use them to access deep potentialities—our compassion, essential wisdom, strength and confidence.

30
TO DANCE AT THE COURT OF INDRA

Our souls are dancers to God; born to dance to God they must enjoy beauty in its perfection. When we forget that dance in our absorption in earthly joys we neglect our duties for which we were created.

Every soul is purposed to dance at the court of Indra.... The one who says: "But how can I dance, I do not know how to dance", he defeats his purpose. For no soul is created to stand aside and look.... Every soul is created to dance at the court of Indra. The soul who refuses certainly shows its ignorance of the great purpose for which this whole play is produced on the earth.[99]

"Homage to Saraswati," performed by Felicia Norton

WE ARE HERE TO UNFOLD THE BUD-LIKE CHRYSALIS of our being. Each day, each moment, our inner and outer lives give us the opportunity to tap the richness of our being and bring forth this beauty, to "dance at the court of Indra," who is, in Indian mythology, the greatest of the gods and the defender of humanity. Indra is connected with fertility, bringing water to the Earth, restoring the parched land to life and affirming an ennobled existence over confusion and despair. In this dance, we are creative and active participants, kindled flames in the evolving universe, in service to the world of "All Possibility."

Dance is a most appropriate symbol of the harvest, the fulfillment or culmination of spiritual development. In indigenous cultures, the harvest is celebrated with dancing. Though rooted in discipline, dance requires freedom, spaciousness and movement, and expresses the interconnectedness of all of life. We have the image of the honeybee moving from flower to flower in a dance of pollination.

One root of the word "dance" translates literally as "to draw towards one." In a Gnostic hymn there is a saying attributed to Christ:

---

[99] Hazrat Inayat Khan, *The Sufi Message of Hazrat Inayat Khan*, Vol. XIV: Sufi Teachings (Geneva: International Sufi Movement, 1963), p. 199.

"Whosoever danceth not, knoweth not the way of life." In the words of the Sufi teacher Samuel Lewis, creator of the Dances of Universal Peace, "The watcher is the prayerful devotee but the dancer becomes divine." Dance is alive and engaged, not sitting on the sidelines as a disappointed observer but involved, in whatever way life asks us, in the joy and struggle of existence. Symbolically, spiritual maturity calls us to go from being a cross-legged, four-pointed figure sitting still in practice, to being a five-pointed star, representing the fullness of a human being engaged in action—standing, moving, and radiating light and life.

Dancing at the court of Indra means becoming a vessel of divine energy, love and grace. Rather than contrived movement, the divine dancer is infused with life's music, with its natural majesty and nobility. This dance serves all of Life, as we offer our being to a hidden but definite choreography, one that calls for our freshness and creativity with each step.

To be a divine dancer requires that we move between different realms of realization, joining heaven and earth. For this we must listen deeply, and then be willing to give all that is asked, not thinking of what effort or cost is expended. This is true prayer, in which any fruits of realization are offered up to the mystery of life. We dance for the Unseen, and it is only the Unseen who can appreciate both our elegant and our sometimes awkward steps. In the words of the Qur'an, "God is beautiful and loves beauty." Our dance is the precious opportunity to contribute something beautiful to the life around us. Manifesting beauty, revealing the splendor of the heavens in this world, is the dancer's work. In whatever way we dance, this affirmation of all that is beautiful is true service to life, and is life-giving and inspiring to the world around us.

The object in the life of the Sufi is to keep the heart like a compass pointing to one goal, the center, Indra for whom every soul is created to dance. We need not go to the forest or the wilderness; we can be in a crowd, but we should be like the compass, always pointing to the one goal of our existence.[100]

---

[100] Hazrat Inayat Khan, *The Sufi Message of Hazrat Inayat Khan*, Vol. XIV: Sufi Teachings (Geneva: International Sufi Movement, 1963), p. 199.

31

A TABLE SPREAD

All our openings and closings, all the beings that we pass through and that pass through us, are gathered together in a single momentous event that is rapidly losing its essential function in our culture. The fundamental event is the Feast. Through it we daily reenact the primordial encounter of inner and outer, where the self meets the other. It is the alchemical event par excellence, in which the substance of things is internalized and transformed. It constitutes our primary engagement with the world.[101]

SHARING A MEAL, A MOST ORDINARY AND UNIVERSAL ACT, has a profound mystical meaning. It joins the infinite to the finite world, our timeless soul partaking in the substance of earthly life. Since antiquity, the feast has been honored in every culture, a symbol of our shared life, and of our sharing in that which is beyond this life. Sharing the table of life with all is the symbol of the peace and well-being of our planet. It brings with it the immediate awareness of and responsibility for people without food and the crucial need to share the bounty we have been given.

From the Arabic word *ma'duba*, meaning banquet, comes the word *adab*, meaning manners. This root sheds another light on the joyous table spread. The beauty of manners is the primary and essential spiritual practice of a mature soul. It echoes Christ's injunction to "love your neighbor as yourself," and this means feeding, clothing and caring for those in need. At another level, it has to do with putting others before us and having respect and generosity towards all. It means overlooking the faults of others, and never seeing others as strangers—every being is a guest at our table.

[101] Tom Cheetham, *Green Man, Earth Angel* (Albany: SUNY Press, 2004), p. 14.

The story of the Last Supper gives us further insight into the feast. Christ's disciples, deeply grieved when they understood that their beloved teacher would be leaving them, feared that they would be lost without his presence. Feeling light, sacredness, and peace when he was with them, they asked their teacher for some concrete way of remembering and holding to the love that they had felt. They were most specific, asking that a "table be spread" for them, as a promise that all the teacher stood for, the welcoming, forgiveness and protection of a benevolent Universe, would still be with them. In response, Christ prayed: "*Lord, Our Sustainer, send down for us a table spread with food from heaven, that it might be an ever-recurring feast for us—for the first and last of us—and a Sign from You. Give us our daily provision, for You are the Best of Providers.*" God said, "*Truly I am sending it down upon you.*"[102]

The bounty of the table spread is so simple, so universal, that its meaning may elude us. Our sharing of connection with all beings, our receiving and giving of the abundant gifts and fruits of this life, confirms in our depths an affirmation by the Unseen. The table spread is a living symbol of a covenant. Like the rainbow it speaks of our unconditional embrace and interpenetration by an intimate and loving Universal Mystery. By this embrace, the simplest and most ordinary activities of this world—the bread and wine of life—take on a most profound significance.

To know that life is a "table spread" before us, we must ourselves know a bounty of spirit. This kind of bounty is realized by an attitude of trust and receptivity. The receptive attitude is symbolized and epitomized by Mary, mother of Jesus, in another story. During a certain period of Mary's youth, Zechariah was given the responsibility of caring for her. But whenever Zechariah entered Mary's solitary chamber, he found that she already had provisions. Mary explained to him that she was being fed by sources unseen, by the Divine Spirit.

Mary is the symbol of the purity and receptivity in our being, the part of us that receives and nurtures the seed of our divinity and ultimately brings us to a new birth. By this our vision of life changes, expands and unfolds, and we are to join and reconciling heaven and earth, our inner and outer lives. Mary also represents the part of us that can surrender to the unknown, letting go and receiving the gifts of each moment.

Trusting in and receiving provision, we are, like Mary, impreg-

[102] Qur'an, Sura 5, Verses 114-15.

nated with seeds from the Divine. By this our highest being comes alive, and we are able to fully claim a life of bounty, of possibility. We can unhesitatingly receive and share the table spread daily before us and fully embrace and appreciate the miracle of this existence.

We can know the table spread most fully as our life shared together, the true bread and wine of a banquet of love and understanding, a simple and most profound reminder of life's covenant with us. We can recognize every table spread as a promise, a shelter and blessing that is offered to us. Accepting each moment, filled sometimes with pain and sometimes with joy, we celebrate the festival of the human journey. By this we truly become the "inheritors of the Earth,", recognizing and grateful for the opportunity each moment brings to us.

This being human
is a guest house,
every morning a new arrival.
A joy, a depression, a meanness,
some momentary awareness comes
as an unexpected visitor.
Welcome and entertain them all!
Even if they are a crowd
of sorrows,
who violently sweep your house
empty of its furniture,
Still treat each guest honorably.
He may be clearing you out for
some new delight.
The dark thought, the sham,
the malice,
Meet them at the door laughing,
and invite them in.
Be grateful for whoever comes,
because each has been sent
as a guide from beyond.[103]

[103] Jelaluddin Rumi, In *The Essential Rumi*, trans. by Coleman Barks. (San Francisco: Harper San Francisco, 1995), p. 109.

32

Serving the Guests

To feed the Angel is to answer for this Divine Mystery who would perish without me, but without whom I should also perish.[104]

"The Trinity", by Andre Rublev, based on the story in the Book of Genesis on the hospitality of Abraham. Some commentators identify the figures as the Archangels Gabriel, Michael and Seraphiel.

WISDOM TELLS US that the maturing soul, beginning to commune with the Unseen Beloved, is faced with a dilemma. The soul begins to longing for union with the Beloved, but also wishes, more than anything, to *please* the Beloved. The bind is that the Beloved wishes not for the ultimate unity, but for the human being to live as a unique individual in this world—resulting in a life in which there must be an inevitable sense of longing and separation. In this regard the great Sufi teacher Al-Alawi observed that "Reality demands a veil". Somehow this veil is needed so that *Ishq*, or ardent desire, may long for and seek its object. Here we can remember the idea that the Divine felt a sense of suffocation when its bounty, beauty and majesty had not yet manifested. In the language of the Sufi, only from true longing did this life—a rose Garden of Mystery and Beauty—come forth. In the same way, by our own longing, the Garden of this life flourishes most fully.

We are here in this world, this rose garden, to recognize and to help others recognize the beauty and majesty of our essential Being. The dimension of helping others is sometimes alluded to within the Sufi tradition through the metaphors of tasting and serving honey. The taste of honey is exquisite, but an even greater pleasure comes in sharing honey with others. In spiritual maturity, we are serving honey, carrying this sweetness right into the middle of life. In this a deeper reality unfolds. Our openness to Reality, and our willingness to serve the

---

[104] Muhyiuddin Ibn Arabi, paraphrased, in Henry Corbin's *Alone with the Alone: Creative Imagination in the Sufism of Ibn Arabi* (Princeton: Bollingen Series XCI, Mythos edition, 1997), p. 316.

life around us, literally gives life to and "nourishes" the Divine in our beings. As such, any act of service within life magnifies and honors the Divine.

The connection of service to spiritual realization is described by Henry Corbin in his interpretation of the story of Abraham's visitation by unexpected guests, depicted above in the image of three angelic figures.[105] The story of the guests is found both in the Book of Genesis and in the Qur'an. The arriving guests appear strange, but Abraham senses immediately their heavenly nature and bows to them with great reverence. He washes their feet and prepares a meal for them.

Corbin sees Abraham's reception of the angels as symbolic of our capacity to realize an "angelic function" in our own beings. He described this function as a capacity to literally nourish or "give life to the Divine", by honoring the sacred in the world around us and in ourselves. As in the story, this begins with a capacity to perceive and recognize the Divine in an unexpected form. Such a recognition is not of an intellectual nature: it requires a pure and luminous consciousness, able to recognize a world of grace and light seeking to reveal itself, to "visit" our everyday experience. It is then by simple and fresh perception that we serve and nourish, or literally give life to the Divine. In turn, we are given new life, receiving a continually deepening capacity to appreciate the miraculous unfolding of life. In Corbin's words, our welcoming—our "angelic function"— allows us to perceive and celebrate a continual and miraculous epiphany, a sacred mystery in every unfolding moment.

---

[105] Corbin's analysis, based largely on the writing of Muhyiuddin Ibn Arabi, is found in *Alone with the Alone: Creative Imagination in the Sufism of Ibn Arabi* (Princeton: Bollingen Series XCI, Mythos edition, 1997), pp. 315-16.

33

SHARING THE GIFT OF AWAKENING

*With bare chest and feet
he enters the market.
his face is smeared with earth,
his head covered with ashes.
A huge laugh streams
over his cheeks.
Without humbling himself to
perform miracles or wonders,
He suddenly makes
the withered trees bloom.*[106]

*Entering the Market with Bliss-
bestowing Hands, by Kuo-an*

THE OX-HERDING PICTURES are a remarkable series of paintings on the stages of the spiritual path. Toward the end of the series is the image here, an adept returning to the market after his spiritual training in the mountains. He comes back, it is said, with "bliss bestowing hands," a generosity and desire to share his realization and freedom. Instead of remaining up in the mountains in solitude, he brings his gifts of spiritual realization to all. Whoever comes into contact with this kind of being receives, either consciously or unconsciously, an energy and light that are beyond description.

Enlightened beings become like giant fruit bearing trees, whose branches both reach up to the sky, to the heavens, and also bow low, laden with nourishing gifts to share with all. Yet beyond concrete gifts and the transmission of energy, these beings remind us that we all must attain their state, and that we all have the capacity to do so. To effect this reminder, these beings do not preach or attempt to convert us to their way of seeing: they simply provide us with a mirror of our own enlightened nature, our true identity.

Hazrat Inayat Khan explains the phenomenon of reflection through a story of a lion and a flock of sheep:

A lion walking through the desert found a little lion cub playing with some sheep. It happened that the little lion had been reared by the sheep,

---

[106] From Kuo-an, #10 of the Ox-Herding Pictures, in *The Ox And The Herdsman*, trans. M.H. Trevor (Tokyo: Hokuseido Press, 1969), pp. 23-24.

and so it had never had a chance or an occasion to realize who it was. The lion was greatly surprised to see the lion cub running away and being just as afraid as the sheep were.

The lion jumped in among the flock of sheep and said, "Halt! Halt!" But the sheep ran away and the little lion ran too. The lion only pursued the lion-cub, and, when it caught up with the cub, the cub said, "I tremble, I am afraid, I cannot stand before you." The lion said, "Why are you running about with the sheep? You yourself are a little lion!" "No," said the little one. "I am a sheep; let me go, let me go with the sheep." "Come along," said the lion, "come with me and I will show you what you are before I let you go." Trembling and yet helpless, the cub followed the lion to the pool of water. Pointing at their reflections in the pool the lion said, "Look at me and look at yourself. Do we not resemble each other closely? You are not like the sheep, you are like me![107]

As the story so well illustrates, the enlightened being provides a clear reflection of our depths. The greatest teacher works in this simple and yet powerful way—not by imposing a belief system but by being a pure mirror of our true nature.

---

[107] Hazrat Inayat Khan, *The Sufi Message of Hazrat Inayat Khan.* Vol. X: Sufi Mysticism (Geneva: International Sufi Movement, 1979), p. 90.

34
THE SURVIVAL ARK

*Humanity is one body, the whole
of life being one in its source and
in its goal, its beginning and its
end. No scientist will deny this.
And if part of the body is in pain,
sooner or later the whole body is
affected; if our finger aches, our
body is not free from pain.*[108]

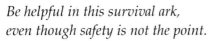

*Be helpful in this survival ark,
even though safety is not the point.
Every guest dies in the end.
But for now, Joseph has been released from prison!*

*Lift your wine in salute to freedom.
Don't be trapped, as others have,
by some quote from the Qur'an.
Abandon, says the rose, and nightingales begin.*[109]

What we discover via spiritual pursuit is not something new, but something we have known and forgotten. Behind the dream of our ordinary experience, and behind the agitation, doubt and fear that we all experience, is a clear field and a wellspring of life-giving waters. But how does the awakening of our natural and essential nature make a difference in this world? What can it have to do, for example with the fact that we are poisoning the body of our Earth — our own greater body, and taking away the freedom of the plants and animals, and children who will come after us?

It may seem unfathomable to us that we can do anything significant to reverse the tremendous environmental damage around us. Yet each of us can do a great deal. Not only can we harness the greatest powers of human ingenuity but we can also align ourselves with forces of goodwill that are immensely powerful. We can be guided, most precisely, by the mysterious wisdom inherent in the Earth, in Nature

[108] Hazrat Inayat Khan, Unpublished paper, *Religious Gathekas #17*, "The Message of Unity."

[109] Hafiz, in *The Hand of Poetry*, trans. Coleman Barks (New Lebanon, NY: Omega Publications, 1993), p. 170.

Herself. As we will see, Hazrat Inayat Khan taught that, in our deepest communication with each other and in our work together, we could tap the very intelligence of our planet and use this most constructively, in small and also in very great ways.

Going forward, a Sufi tale can help us. This classic story, from Attar's *The Conference of the Birds,* begins:

All the birds of the world, known and unknown, assembled together and declared a need to find the king of birds, the "Simurgh." They said: "No country in the world is without a king. How came it, then, that the kingdom of the birds is without a ruler? This state of things cannot last. We must make an effort together and search for one; for no country can have a good administration and a good organization without a king."[110]

Thousands of birds set out on the search for the King. They go through tremendous tests and trials, far beyond anything that they thought they could withstand. Years and years are spent in valleys of longing, doubt and fear as they struggle and drag themselves towards their destination. Through this long and winding teaching story, Attar masterfully outlines the stages and struggles of the spiritual journey.

Only thirty birds reach the King's palace. Even there the trials continue, as the chamberlain at first refuses the birds entry. After much insisting and lamenting, the survivors are led to the throne room. With great anticipation they take seats around the throne and wait for the King. First hours and then many days are spent in waiting, but no King arrives. Finally, abandoning all hope, the birds go into deep meditation. After a long time, they open their eyes. The throne remains empty, but they suddenly are drawn to look into each other's eyes. Attar narrates:

In the reflection of each other's faces, these thirty birds of the outer world contemplated the face of the Simurgh of the inner world. This so astonished them that they did not know if they were still themselves or if they had become the Simurgh. At last, in a state of contemplation, they realized that they were the Simurgh and that the Simurgh was the thirty birds.... They realized that they and the Simurgh were one and the same being. No one in the world has ever heard of anything equal to it.[111]

As we reflect on our deepest identity, we remember what the

[110] Farid Ud-Din Attar, *The Conference of the Birds,* trans. C.S. Nott (New York: Samuel Weiser, 1954), p. 11.

[111] Farid Ud-Din Attar, ibid, p. 131.

great teachers have told us, that we are truly one body, and that, when any part of this body is suffering or troubled, we are all affected. With this understanding, we must listen and seek out ways to help healing come to every cell, every atom of our one Body.

Working within the collective dream of our existence, we can touch the possibility of restoring our world. When we learn to truly communicate with each other, doors open—possibilities emerge, and solutions to problems become apparent. Instead of seeing the modern world, with its emphasis on technology and science as demonic, we can realize that tremendous potential is present that must be mustered and intelligently guided. Used with wisdom, the very same things that are now poisoning us can help to feed people and foster health.

Our deep communication over the problems of our Earth can not only will help us solve our problems but also be a most powerful force for planetary awakening. Hazrat Inayat Khan observes:

> *The Planet has culminated in human beings. There is a gradual awakening of matter to become conscious... In matter life unfolds, discovers and realizes that consciousness that has been buried in it for thousands of years....*
>
> *The collective working of many minds as one single idea, and the activity of the whole world, are governed by the intelligence of the planet and unlock the doors opening up into a glorious future. The thought of any person is the thought of the entire human race. The whole universe has contributed to the way humanity thinks today. The experience of every soul becomes the experience of the divine mind. Not knowing that Universal Being experiences this life through the human being, [we are] seeking for Her/Him somewhere else.* [112.]

The "work" that is in front of us—the cultivation of a field that can provide the harvest and seed for the future—is a most profound and most exciting venture. Relatively speaking, our limited minds and fragile bodies have only a few brief moments to address this work while here. And while we indeed have very far to go, the need to realize our capacities to communicate in a profound and meaningful way is something we are beginning to recognize. A first step is the art of community dialogue as it has been brought into our awareness by physicist

---

[112] Hazrat Inayat Khan, in Pir Vilayat Khan, *In Search of the Hidden Treasure* (New York: Tarcher, 2003), p. 184.

David Bohm.[113] We need to see ourselves as a sacred community, recognizing the divine in each other. Like the "thirty birds" looking for Reality, we discover it in each other, realizing who we are collectively and, affirming a shared purpose, allowing new possibilities for being and living to emerge.

[113] David Bohm made initial strides to develop a form of non-hierarchical dialogue that allows for a profound sharing of insights, sentiments and ideas. Variants of his work are used today in many arenas of life. See *On Dialogue*, by David Bohm (London: Routledge, 1996).

35
A Universe Seeking Beauty

O my Beloved, I ask you for a swift reunion with Creative Beauty, impregnable Majesty and exalted Perfection, in every state and in every outcome.[114]

LIFE SEEKS BEAUTY, evolves towards beauty and ever finds new ways to manifest beauty. And while this appears a most radical alternative to prevailing belief, each of us in our depths knows this truth. Yet to go from an attractive philosophical idea to a reality in our everyday life appears a very big step. But let us look more deeply into the vision that reveals this hidden code. For this we turn to the writings of Chuang Tsu, a great Taoist master. It is the story of Master Kheng and the carving of a bell stand.

Kheng, the master carver, made a bell stand
of precious wood. When it was finished,
all who saw it were astounded.
They said it must be the work of spirits.
The Prince of Lu said to the master carver;
"What is your secret?" Kheng replied: "I am only a workman;
I have no secret. There is only this:
When I began to think about the work you commanded,
I guarded my spirit,
did not expend it on trifles, that were not to the point.
I fasted in order to set my heart at rest. After three days fasting,
I had forgotten gain and success.
After five days I had forgotten praise or criticism.
After seven days I had forgotten my body with all its limbs.
By this time all thought of your Highness

[114] Muhyiuddin Ibn Arabi, *The Seven Days of the Heart, Prayers for the Nights and Days of the Week,* trans. Pablo Beneito and Stephen Hirtenstein (Oxford: Anqa Publishing, 2000), p. 137.

And of the court had faded away.
All that might distract me from my work had vanished.
I was collected in the single thought of the bell stand.
Then I went to the forest to see the trees
in their own natural state.
When the right tree appeared before my eyes,
the bell stand also appeared in it, clearly, beyond doubt.
All I had to do was put forth my hand and begin.
If I had not met this particular tree
there would have been no bell stand at all.
What happened? My own collected thought
encountered the hidden potential in the wood;
From this live encounter came the work
which you ascribe to the spirits."[115]

This story, seemingly about a bygone era and a faraway land, is truly about our lives. It tells of the secret of Creative Beauty, how this beauty reveals Herself to us and asks our participation, It urges us to make ourselves ready and gives us the proper lens by which we may also see this beauty in any circumstance.

Like Master Kheng, a fierce honesty is needed. We have to see beyond praise and blame, beyond the distracting trifles of wealth, fame and position. We need to concentrate our being, mustering all our energy and faith for the purpose of bringing forth creative vision and encountering our life with this vision. It was similar actions that enabled Kheng to see, within the trunk of a forest tree, the potential for the exquisite bell stand.

The key to beauty—both in Master Kheng's story and in ourselves—is the recognition of potential. Seeing what *could be* takes us beyond the limitation of all that is false, all that might be obscuring our vision. The challenges that are presented to us in our everyday life are much like Kheng's. Our life *is* the bell stand, revealing its beauty when we put our fullest concentration in our work, and when we are able to extricate ourselves from habits of judgment, blame and praise. The fruit of this effort is attained when we tune our hearts and consciousness to the depths of our being, learning to work with Creative Beauty as it emerges in our life.

[115] Chuang Tzu, in *The Way of Chuang Tzu*, by Thomas Merton (New York: New Directions Publishing, 1965), pp. 110-11.

36

CREATIVE BEAUTY—THE WAY OF SOPHIA

Sophia represents the wisdom of the Earth; Wisdom is the Divine Intelligence that fertilizes the Earth.[116]

THE WORLD OF BEAUTY AND POSSIBILITY is the noblest dream of consciousness. It is not simply a human dream, though it arises within us in both waking and sleeping states. It is the power that brought us here, that created this life as a fertile field of unlimited potentialities. In this dream, the Hidden Beloved is calling out to us to be aware, to see possibilities, to recognize and align ourselves with the beauty that wishes to unfold. This is the possibility of an earth of beauty, an Emerald Earth. This is the purpose of our journey to this life. A Divine spark from the world of splendor is within us, yearning to recognize itself in the mirror of the created world.

This "dream of possibility" is written into our psyches and souls. Here, in the voice of Sophia in the Book of Proverbs, it is expressed as the passion of the Divine to live and play with the children of the Earth:

The Holy One possessed me in the beginning of the way
before the works of old.
I was poured out from Eternity,
from the beginning before earth was.
When there were no depths, I was brought forth,
when there were no springs abounding with water.
Before the mountains were settled,
before the hills was I brought forth,
while as yet he had not made the earth, nor the fields,

[116] Pir Vilayat Khan, *Relationships, Energy and Elements*, Recorded talk. (New Lebanon, NY: Sufi Order International, 1986).

nor the highest part of the clay of the world.
When he prepared the heavens, I was there,
when he set a compass upon the face of the depth;
when he established the clouds above,
when he strengthened the fountains of the deep,
when he gave to the sea his bound,
that the waters should not pass his commandment,
when he appointed the foundations of the earth,
then I was by him, as one brought up with him;
and I was daily his delight, rejoicing always before him,
rejoicing in the habitable part of his earth,
and my delights were with the children of the Earth.
                                    —Proverbs 8:22-31

The being of Sophia, as the voice of Wisdom, was dear to writer and mystic Thomas Merton, who since childhood knew her as Proverb and found joy in her songs. At a certain crucial moment in his life, Merton remembered the feeling he had as a child when reading her words. Having long separated himself from the world, and also finding something missing in his exclusively "spiritual" vision of life, Merton began to dream of Proverb/Sophia. The dreams prefigured a moment of clarity and insight in which his view shifted radically (and, as we described earlier, came after his touching the ground of being, *le pointe verge*, in his meditation):

In Louisville, at the corner of Fourth and Walnut, in the center of the shopping district, I was suddenly overwhelmed with the realization that I loved all these people, that they were mine and I theirs, that we could not be alien to one another even though we were total strangers. It was like waking from a dream of separateness.... [117]

Describing this experience to Boris Pasternak, Merton wrote,

Suddenly I saw that everybody was Proverb and that all of them shone her extraordinary beauty and purity and shyness, even though they did not know who they were and perhaps were ashamed of their names because they were mocked on account of them. And they did not know their real identity as the Child so dear to God who, from before the beginning,

[117] Thomas Merton, *Conjectures of a Guilty Bystander* (New York: Doubleday, 1989), pp. 156-57.

147

was playing in His sight all days, playing in the world....[118]

The secret of life is revealed in the fulfillment of the passion of Sophia, the Divine embrace of our "ordinary" life on earth. It requires our self-acceptance, and a reconciliation of our childlike innocence, beauty and purity with our humanness. It is through this reconciliation, made while remaining engaged with life's drama, that we can fully appreciate the precious gift of each moment in this world.

In truth, the impulse of Sophia-Wisdom to "delight with the children of the Earth," is the deepest desire of our own soul. By serving the life in front of us, by bringing forth Creative Beauty, we realize that this Reality is the living body and soul of the Divine. Reality—who is this Sophia—lives and experiences life through us and, at the same time, is at home in the heart of Universal Love.

Sophia fulfills Her passion, and also brings our ultimate satisfaction, in the dance of our lives, seeking Creative Beauty and its unfolding in every domain. She urges us to listen, to trust in Her ways. She calls us to open the doors of our hearts, to come to our senses, to help each other and thereby embrace our connection with all of life on our precious Emerald Earth. She beckons us:

Climb out of the prison! Live!
Be my Love, my Compassion! Walk, with my Power,
Dance, in my Beauty! Delight in my Body, Your Earth!

---

[118] Thomas Merton, *Six Letters: Boris Pasternak, Thomas Merton,* Naomi B. Stone ed. (Lexington, KY: University of Kentucky, 1973), pp. 11-12.

PRACTICES — THE HARVEST

The practices for the harvest are active ones, aimed at enhancing energy, insight and creativity for use in everyday situations and for the ultimate purpose of contributing to the world around us. They are used to cast light on all situations and to become the mature caretakers and cultivators of creation.

Practice #17: Concentration Practice: Life Energy

The universe is continually dispensing new life. The play of elements makes possible a continual dispensation of life energy into our world. This energy is called *Prana* in Sanskrit, *Hayy* in Arabic, or *Chaim* in Hebrew, all of which literally mean "Life." A similar recognition of life energy is used by many indigenous traditions around the world.

To concentrate on this outpouring of life energy is to commune with it. It is like high-voltage energy, quickening and animating our bodies, hearts and souls. It is a streaming life current, the energy of birth and the feeling of a raw encounter with nature.

Concentrating on life energy activates our own being and the life around us. This energy has a progressive aspect, allowing us to move forward into new realms. In the very depths of our being, we can sense our nature to be pure "life," and know that, despite outer appearances, we are moved by the very same energy that moves the universe. To the degree we realize this, we are better conduits of life energy, enhancing the continual infusion and nourishment of the world around us with magnetism and life.

1. Contemplate the raw energies of life. Think of the power and energy that manifest in the motion of the sun, moon and planets, or in the sap rising in the trees. Realize this same life force moves

149

continually through our beings.

2. Inhale and tune your consciousness to the subtle life energy infusing your entire being, feeling connected to every molecule of the universe. Attune to enlivening, pulsating life energy. Exhale and feel your cells tingling and activated with this energy, the same whirling energy that moves the planets and galaxies. You could repeat silently the word "Hayy" or "Life" on the inhalation and on the exhalation.

3. Investigate and observe what in your experience enhances this life energy and what depletes it. Feel your regard for the sanctity of all life. Honor each being—human, animal, plant and mineral— as a living manifestation of Divine Life. Tune in to the life energy that brings things to fruition and brings creation into full manifestation.

As a Walking Practice

Breathe in through the soles of the feet, inhaling the restorative energy rising from Earth. Breathe in pure spirit, celestial energy, from above the crown of the head, allowing it to descend. Tune your awareness to a regenerating energy rising from within, recharging your being. Exhale and radiate life-giving energy in every direction.

Further Variations

1. To enhance awareness of life energy, visualize water flowing. Imagine yourself under a waterfall, the powerful and life-giving energy pouring through your being. This practice is especially helpful in the middle of a difficult situation in which there appears to be no movement. Imagine this water flowing, washing away and dissolving obstacles, or imagine your own being as the water of a moving river, flowing around obstacles.

2. Visualize a river flowing from left to right, representing movement from the past into the future. You may move the head from the left to the right shoulder, and experience the movement of a powerful, slow current, carrying energy and richness into manifestation. This practice brings latent potentialities into existence.

3. Feel your heart as a miniature sun, radiating and overflowing with love for all beings.

Practice #18: Newly Emerging Buds Of Potential

As we discussed early in the book, many scientists and mystics will agree that every moment, the universe appears "in a new configuration." Nothing stays exactly the same, in spite of our attempts to hold on to our familiar picture of life. The gift in this is that *we* are never the same, either. In each moment, we are literally created anew. This practice will help us to gain access to this sense of continual rebirth, and

thereby to bring out the fresh potentialities that are ever arising within us.

1. An ancient Sufi practice is to use the breath to recognize the present moment as a sharp sword, cutting through impressions of the past, such as of betrayal, guilt or resentment, and also through our grasping towards the future. Draw in breath to bring yourself to the freshness of the present. Using the moment of the holding of the breath to allow creativity to rise up from within, unfolding new potentialities. As you exhale, let your essence bring forth a new dispensation of vitalizing energy and light, radiating in all directions.

2. Now imagine a flower with its many petals. Feel your being as this flower. Envision all the outer petals in their beauty and manifestation, along with the bud inside, ready to open with fresh life. Imagine allowing the outer petals that have outlived their usefulness to release. Something new will emerge from the center of the flower, from the freshness of the bud.

3. Breathe in and briefly hold the breath. As you suspend the breath, release the pull of your fixed identity. It is here, in the suspension of the breath, that we can sense the latent possibilities within the bud, waiting to flower. Sensing all this potential allows it to be brought forth.

4. Holding to negative impressions is a way of self-deception. Focusing on mistakes, shortcomings and guilt make our path more difficult and actually feeds resistance to unfolding. While acknowledging of wrongdoing is crucial, dwelling on regrets wrongly convinces us that we are the same person we were in the last moment. There is nothing in our experience that requires us to hold on to who we were. This also relates to painful emotions, which, once felt, need not captivate us. We can simply let ourselves and others off the hook, finding new life in our being.

5. Accenting the moment of held breath, we feel the blossoming of our being, as expectancy, freshness and light. Let the light within the heart act as a catalyst, opening to the depths of being. Imagine that this light acts on the tender bud and brings forth the bloom of a fresh flower. As the outer petals fall away, feel the bud opening, new energy emerging as new potentialities come into life. Sense a fragrance and freshness emitted from the center of the bud.

There is a story from India that symbolizes the way our consciousness can act upon the life around us. In the story, a garden is dry and parched. As Prince Puran walks through the garden, his very presence and magnetism trigger new life, the blooming and fruitfulness of the flowers and trees. The same dynamic happens when we are in harmony within and without: we become life-giving, most naturally and not by any effort of the will. Simply being our natural selves, what comes through us quickens the life around us, the effect akin to seeds being watered. New life and new possibilities arise in an environment charged with energy, insight, light and magnetism.

Practice #19: Meditation on the Shekinah

Collected bits of truth
Shimmering sparks
  Shards of light
Merge
  Healing
  Restoring
  Bursting Bright
Rising
  in divine ecstatic flame.[119]

The mystery of the Shekinah touches every seeking soul. In the Song of Solomon, she is the feminine face of Divine Mystery, the Beloved. In the Qur'an, *sakina* is the indwelling spirit of peace and grace, descending on the devotee as a felt Presence. As *indwelling*, this being and presence stirs our appreciation for the glory embodied in this life — its light, shelter, beauty and peace.

Shekinah as a presence was recognized and protected in the Ark of the Covenant and in the tabernacle of Solomon's temple. Within the Kabbalah, She represents the nurturing force of the entire Earth, flowing into creation, the Divine Presence on earth.

At the center of the tabernacle of our heart, in the Holy of Holies, Shekinah is the torch of light that casts light on any darkness in this world. As the ordering principle behind Creation, Shekinah is the Beauty and Glory that become our own ordering principles when we open and receive Her as a truly living presence. Also recognized as the Sabbath bride who unites two worlds, She descends at sunset on the eve of the Sabbath, enfolding the world in peace and tranquility. In Her embrace, the world becomes a Holy Field, where male and female join in sacred lovemaking. This union is the *hieros-gamos*, the union of heaven and earth, spirit and matter.

The imagery of Shekinah as the Sabbath bride is not an abstraction but a symbol of an attainable realization. It captures something of the magic of Her unexpected descent into our ordinary experience, affirming the depths of every soul who perseveres in the sacred work

[119] Nimoy, Leonard, *Shekhina* (New York: Umbrage Editions, 2002), p. 81.

of reflecting heaven on earth.

1. In this practice open your hands, palms facing upwards, as a gesture of becoming fully receptive and open to receiving the gift of sacredness, of sacred Presence. This presence comes without strings and not as a result of our worthiness. While this gift is always present, the tests and struggles of our life distract us, and we often miss what is being given.

2. Making it a practice to simply be open to Shekinah's presence, feel your anxieties and fears washed away, and realize a state of "pure affirmation" in which there is nothing to fear. Grace and peace surround and protect you.

3. Open yourself, prepare yourself, for the descent of the Holy Presence of Shekinah. Imagination is a bridge to the reality of this being. Open to luminosity, grace, beauty and protection, the Shekinah's very atmosphere. Think of the meaning of the Sabbath, in which we rest, suspending our striving and opening to receive the holy celebration as it descends.

4. Feel the sacredness underlying all of existence, the fullest embrace of heaven and earth, around you and inside of you as well. The contact with Shekinah puts us in touch not only with clarity and peace, but with strength and inner guidance. She is the very spirit of guidance.

5. See yourself opening again and again to the peace and calm of the Shekinah in the midst of your life. Recognize the holy infusion of light that She brings. Seeing beyond agitation, remember Her in the middle of daily struggles, trusting that calm and peace can be restored and can prevail, and that greater and greater beauty can ever be revealed.

Practice #20: Reading Nature's Manuscript

When the eyes and ears are open, the leaves of the tree become as a sacred living manuscript.[120]

There comes a time with the maturity of the soul when every thing and every being begins to reveal its nature to us.... We know then that this wide nature is ever-revealing and that one can always communicate with it. Many souls remain blind with open eyes. They are in heaven, but not allowed to look at heaven. They are in paradise, but not allowed to enjoy the beauties of paradise. It is just like a person sleeping on a pile of gems and jewels. From the moment man's eyes open and he begins to read the book of nature he begins to live; and he continues to live forever.[121]

We are here to realize our deepest identity. Who and what we are cannot be grasped with our theories or philosophies. Yet when we are willing to open most fully to our experience, we can taste the truth of our lives. As we gain intimacy with our own depths, nature will speak to each of us, in most unique ways. We can make it a practice to "witness" this communication, without preconception and without even attempting to describe what we experience.

We truly are sleeping on a pile of gems, very often totally unaware of the treasure that this life is offering us. The Earth mirrors the riches inside of us, the priceless treasure of our humanness. Life waits for us to realize this treasure, to witness, communicate and embrace it. The wind whispers and inspires, and signals moments of change. The thunder and lightning humble us and open us to a state of awe. The rose calls us, most intimately, to come close, to take in its sweet scent and vivid color. Thrilled by our gaze, the rose is affirmed and fulfilled.

When we are awake in the way a child is awake to the magic of a

---

[120] Hazrat Inayat Khan, *The Sufi Message of Hazrat Inayat Khan*, Vol. IX: The Unity of Religious Ideals (Geneva: International Sufi Movement, 1963) p. 239.

[121] Hazrat Inayat Khan, *The Sufi Message of Hazrat Inayat Khan*. Vol. XIII: Philosophy, Psychology and Mysticism (Geneva: International Sufi Movement, 1982), pp. 172-73.

garden, everything communicates with us. Everything points back to our true identity. In Persian one name for the Divine is *Khuda*, which literally means "The Self-Revealing One." The emerald has a particularly strong quality of "self-revelation" of ineffable beauty. When our hearts are clear, every moment and every aspect of the natural world offers us its self-revelation. The beauty, mercy and gifts of creation only require appreciative eyes.

The practice here is a meditation with open eyes, a simple fresh awareness that the world revealing itself in front of us is Universal Mystery, Creative Beauty seeking itself in a mirror. Work with this thought in nature at first, but ultimately in each and every situation. See beauty when it is present, but also think of the potential for beauty even in its absence. See with gratitude and openness, shedding any tendency to analyze, assess or judge. Realize that you are, when seeing through an appreciative lens, the very eyes of the Universe, gazing upon itself. Turn your gaze, again and again, to Creative Beauty, and allow the depths of your being to "read" the sacred manuscript of nature.

Practice #21: The Fulfillment of the Soul's Desire

Let Thy wish become my desire.
Let Thy will become my deed,
Let Thy word become my speech, Beloved,
And Thy love become my creed.
Let my plant bring forth Thy flowers,
Let my fruits produce Thy seed,
Let my heart become Thy lute, Beloved,
And my body Thy flute of reed. [122]

Our embodiment on Earth is immensely meaningful. However unfathomable it may be, the universe is enriched, for all eternity, through each human being's unique journey through life. For we *are* the universe, in its journey of awakening. And it is within our life, with all its ups and down, and within our pain, errors and great joys, that the universe recognizes itself. Our life, in its every detail, gives shape and form to a universe in the process of awakening.

The soul is an action of the Divine. We connect most deeply to

[122] Hazrat Inayat Khan, *Complete Sayings, Gayan* (New Lebanon, NY: Sufi Order Publications, 1978), p. 101.

this action, this energy, through desire as it arises in our heart. Every desire reflects the original desire, the *Ishq*, meaning Love, Divine Passion, directed towards manifestation, towards fulfillment. It is Love that acts as a gravity, compelling a ray of the Divine to leave a place of unity and perfection, to descend into matter, becoming life itself. *Ishq*, as the energy behind our every desire, also reflects our original covenant, our willingness to incarnate as an act of glory. For this reason, nothing can fulfill our soul more than coming to this Earth, with all its problems and limitations, and here realizing and manifesting the Divine.

Can we remember our true passion and pledge to embody the splendor of Being while on Earth? Can we allow our souls to be rekindled, and thereby realize the resurrection of the Earth in this very moment?

Our conscious affirmation that we are here to unfold our potentialities and beauty, to bring splendor to earth, brings us a deep sense of excitement and satisfaction. Though the link is not always immediately clear, this unfolding positively affects the world around us, and is intricately connected to our survival on this planet. Simply stated, it provides an accommodation in which the Divine can most fully reveal Intelligence, Wisdom and Presence to this world.

Hazrat Inayat Khan emphasized that if our desire is not fulfilled in this world, it is because we did not truly know *how* to desire. Here, beginning with an awareness that our desire reflects the impulse of the Divine to touch the Earth, we use our intimacy with the elements, and their energy and power, to unfold the fullness of our being.

The attunements and imagery associated with earth, water, fire, air and ether are used to support and affirm the fulfillment of our desire. Specifically, we use the qualities associated with the elements to bring these deepest yearnings into manifestation.

Here we will be reversing the order of the elements as previously introduced, this time starting with the ether, and then coming from vast space, descending from the air through the fire and water elements. Ultimately our practice concludes with the earth element, and with fully grounding our desire on Earth.

1. To begin, totally relax and reconnect with the original impulse that brought you to earth. Why are you here and what is truly most important to you? We begin with ether, a sense of being home in the spacious realms of non-form. Breathing very subtly in and out of the nose, feel a state of pure potential.

2. Next, Work with the air element, attuning to the soul's deepest wish. The air breath is in and out the mouth. Here we experience desire as the soul's wish, its nostalgia to manifest something beautiful, profound or original, its yearning for fulfillment.

3. Making this wish more manifest, we enter the realm of the fire element. The fire breath is in the mouth and out the nose. Experience passion, enthusiasm and ardor as your wish heats into a blaze, transformed into desire. When more acquainted with our desire, we become one with passion, on fire with energy, lit up and alive with the power to accomplish.

4. As our desire comes more into life we enter the water element. Here energy flows downward into manifestation. We inhale through the nose and exhale through the mouth. This is a flowing state, filled with hope and faith. Water can move around obstacles flowing to its destination. Water can also carve rock. Our desire becomes will. Always in movement, and as a current under the earth, water has a tremendous power to finds its way.

5. Finally we come to the earth element, where we concretize our will. Breathe in and out the nose. The element of earth gives forbearance, patience and endurance in accomplishing our task. What began as our amorphous wish in the realm of the air element became a flame of desire, then flowed with purpose through water and now is concretized in the realm of the earth element. The earth provides the accommodation, the living ground for desire to take root, grow and be accomplished.

Practice #22: Nourishing the Field of Our Being

There is a stream which is constantly in touch with the depth; this is the mystic life. [123]

The guidance from the outer knowledge and the guidance from the inner intelligence are both necessary. If the inner light were enough, then man would never have been created; he would have been an angel. [124]

Two seemingly opposite forces continually pull upon us. We are drawn towards transcendent Mystery and, at the very same time, towards our life in the world. We can easily feel that these directions are at odds with each other. The call of the transcendent realm fulfills a yearning in the soul to rise above all, to be at one with the Source of life, to retreat into the unity, peace and solitude of being. The call to immanence, to our life in this world, fulfills a longing for attainment and manifestation. This latter pull is the *Ishq*, the original and cosmic desire of the soul to descend from unity into life. The *Ishq* expresses the joy of engagement, of love's longing to manifest, leaving peace and unity for satisfaction and enrichment.

In truth, our desires for peace and joy, for transcendence and immanence, are expressions of the very same Reality. They come into conflict when we want one without remaining open to the other, and when we do not honor both as crucially important. For this reason a great wandering Sufi sage, Baba Kule, is said to have cried in perplexity: *"When I am lost in the Divine Immanence, God reveals His/Her Transcendence. When I am lost in the Divine Transcendence, God reveals His/Her Immanence."*

1. On the out-breath, we extend into the realm of existence, of manifestation. On the in-breath, we return to the source of Being, infinite and abstract, transcending the struggles of life, renewing our being at the "still point of the turning world." The out-breath extends again into the world of manifestation as a breath of compassion.

2. The seeming contradiction of the abstract and manifest dimensions of consciousness is resolved by the understanding that our sense of separation in this world is an illusion. The image of the

[123] Hazrat Inayat Khan, unpublished papers.

[124] Hazrat Inayat Khan, *Supplementary Papers*, "Inner Guidance" (New Lebanon, NY: Sufi Order International, 1966).

lotus informs us: many seemingly separate leaves and flowers appear on the surface of a lake, but these are connected to the same root under the water.

3. The in-breath expresses the vertical or transcendent dimension, linking the individual to the universal, the unity of being. The out-breath, reaching all of manifestation, is the horizontal dimension. The practice is best done at first in silence and with eyes closed. As familiarity develops, the same essential practice can be maintained in everyday life with eyes open.

Here, in one full inhalation and exhalation, we experience unity at its source, overflowing into life, our boundless nature moving into and through life. Through the breathing we sense the resolution of the seemingly opposite pulls: We can be fully engaged with life without feeling a sense of separation. We can see beyond the appearances of separation, and can touch a sense of a continuity. We can touch and feel the very Source of life as a backdrop of love and bliss, ever seeking to infuse the world. This Source is at once the root intricately connected to each being and circumstance, and is the flowing water that revivifies and nourishes every domain of life.

Joining Transcendence and Immanence

First Stage: Emphasis on transcendence.

1. Allow the notion of individuality to dissolve. In the void beyond space and time, feel replenished and purified of all the bonds of material existence, all the intricacies and messiness of life. Feel buoyancy, realizing the spaces between the molecules of your being.

2. Feel the weight of your life circumstances, your regrets and plans all lifted from you. You are pure, free, made whole again: "The boisterous rivers are becalmed when they reach the ocean and feel their union."[125] *Go beyond yourself: expand into clear and empty sky, attuning to vastness and freedom, peace and unity.*

Second Stage: Emphasis on existence.

1. Start with a gentle breath inhaled and exhaled. Inhale. Then

[125] Attributed to Muinuddin Chishti.

160

*hold your breath in a state of suspension, drawing your con-
sciousness up to the third eye and the crown center, where all
the divine potentialities are waiting to come forth. On the out-
breath be the midwife of divine qualities—love, creativity, joy,
freshness and insight, bringing these into existence.*

2. *Again on the inhalation, touch on the innermost depths of
being, the black light of the solar plexus. Exhale from what is
emerging within, and recognize that you are literally giving birth
to new being. Let this birth come forth, free of the past, fresh in
the moment. What do you sense wishes to come through at this
moment? Realize that you do not have to wait for years for the
proper circumstances to arrive to bring about change. Transformation can be initiated by a gentle breath, in and out, making a
bridge between the potentialities arising from your depths and
outer reality.*

3. *On the out-breath, feel united with all in existence. Reflect on
the thought that the One Being, out of a yearning to manifest love
and beauty, left the solitude and perfection of unity, fragmenting
into this world of duality, descending on a breath of compassion
and creating life as we know it. This is the ever-renewed* **Ishq***, the
desire of the One to manifest and find itself here as love, harmony
and beauty. As you exhale, feel this force of love leaving the solitude of peace to become the joy of manifestation and existence.
Feel freshness, new creation emerging from every breath, like a
wave of the ocean breaking towards the shore. Each breath, having been purified and resorbed into unity, expands and literally
incarnates as a force for enrichment and revivification of life.*

*In this most simple practice, take the time to express gratitude
for each breath. Just a single moment of full presence is extraordi-
narily beautiful, charged with revelation and great love. In such
a moment, a simple sound, that of the wind or of a bell, can trigger a state of ecstasy. Softening and deepening, listen to the universal sound in all.*

*Breathing into our source, we touch pure consciousness, redis-
covering itself and finding renewal in its eternal home. Exhaling,
we breathe splendor, beauty and magnanimity into life.*

Practice #23: True Vision—The Creative Glance

The only real voyage or discovery consists not in seeking new landscapes but in having new eyes.[126]

The Presence of Imagination—which we have called the Meeting Place of the Two Seas—embodies meanings and subtilizes the sensory object. It transforms the entity of every object of knowledge in the viewer's eye.[127]

We have lifted the veil from you so that your sight is today keen.

—*Qur'an Sura 50, Verse 22*

What is true vision? It is seeing through the myriad veils of this life to what lies hidden, beyond separateness to an underlying unity and splendor. True seeing is free of distortions, impressions and bias. It begins always with a freshness, the fruit of deep meditation.
Vision is the key factor in determining what unfolds in our lives. With wisdom and practice we come to realize that sight does not simply mean being passive or taking on impressions, but rather casting the light of our Soul upon all, and especially upon all that may be dark or unclear in our lives.

Meditation with Open Eyes

Not all the knowledge learned from books and from experiences in the world and collected in the mind as learning is wisdom. When the light from within is thrown upon this knowledge, then the knowledge from outer life and the light coming from within make a perfect wisdom; and it is that wisdom which guides the human being on the path of life.[128]

In the section on the ground of being, we turned consciousness deeply within, touching what the Sufis call the light of intelligence, a

[126] Marcel Proust in J. O'Brien, ed. *The Maxims of Marcel Proust* (New York: Columbia University Press, 1948), p. 181.

[127] Muhyiuddin Ibn Arabi, quoted in William Chittick, *The Sufi Path of Knowledge* (Albany, SUNY Press, 1989), p. 89.

[128] Hazrat Inayat Khan, *The Sufi Message of Hazrat Inayat Khan*, Vol. IV: Mental Purification (Geneva: International Sufi Movement, 1961) p. 228.

light that exists independently of form and of consciousness. Here we emphasize bringing this light into our lives. With a regular practice of cleansing our perception and thinking, removing the many layers of impressions that cloud our vision, we develop a glance that is active rather than passive, that radiates light and splendor. This particular light does not require the force of will power or ego, but naturally illuminates, catalyzes and transforms the life around us.

It takes much concentration to meditate with open eyes. While this is a very advanced practice, it is one that we can gradually become adept at. The relationship of our physical eyes to our thinking is literally hard-wired. As soon as we open our eyes after an internal meditation, all the objects in the physical environment call out for our attention. Therefore, for this particular meditation with open eyes, we have to literally retrain our consciousness so that it is not pulled in every direction.

1. The method of meditation with open eyes should be prefaced by a time of deep meditation with eyes closed. We first charge our being with the light of intelligence and the emotion of the splendor that is behind life. We can first tune to the emotion that originally created life. Then we can reflect on the abstract, the inner, eternal plane of the soul, the world that transpires behind the world of appearances. Once we are doing this, we are ready to open our eyes and meditate into life. Ideally, it is best to do this practice first in nature (or, if we cannot be in nature, to give our attention first to natural objects such as plants, crystals, the sky, etc.).

2. For further development of this meditation, we practice intensely turning our gaze inward. We notice that, even when our eyes are closed, they are oriented forward and outward. Turn attention inward and upward towards the third eye (located in the space between the eyebrows), converging light at a point. With enough practice, we may see flashes—sometimes brilliant flashes—of light at the third eye. Whether or not we see these, concentrating deeply on the third eye has the effect of charging the eyes with the light of the heavenly spheres. Here reflect on the words of Hazrat Inayat Khan, "Look up first, and when your eyes are charged with divine light, then when you cast your glance on the world of facts you will have a much clearer vision, the vision of reality." Then, opening our eyes, we can offset our glance slightly from the physical world. This will help keep us from being pulled too strongly by the attraction of objects. Next, we can experience looking upon our life with our whole body and mind. We are like a sun, gazing at the life around us and realizing it to be a mirror of our light. We cast a creative glance, giving light to the world. We hold in mind the thought of being transparent to the light and life energy that come through us into life.

3. The creative glance is compassionate but diamond-like, penetrating the covers and veils of the separate existence in which we normally function. Looking into life, we are carrying awareness of the Divine presence to each moment. In that presence is a sense of the sacred, but also of vastness, bliss and fulfillment.

4. All of life, and millions of years of evolution, comes to fruition through this glance. As light streams through our eyes, it radiates to all of matter. Filled with light, our physical eyes, our third eye and our hearts communicate illumination. As this practice comes alive within us, we are naturally and effortlessly casting light into the life around us—rather than simply absorbing the light that comes from the environment. The cells of our being dance with light, radiating in infinite directions.

When we truly concentrate on and enhance the light in our being, we are serving our primordial pledge to "be of service to the transfiguration of the world." Casting light, not by an active force of the ego but by a simple transparency and generous attitude, makes all the difference in our life, contributing to an uplifted world. Most subtly this light provides guidance and clarity to all those whom we encounter. In a metaphor used by Hazrat Inayat Khan, it is like a certain lantern that the farmer carries into a field on a dark night, lighting the way. This lantern, illuminating us within and without, reminds us of our long forgotten identity—our connection to the source of Being— and brings mercy and compassion, freedom and joy to this life, serving the manifestation of Creative Beauty.

Extension—A Rainbow of Light

1. A further development of this practice is to begin with a meditation on the rainbow of light, as in the Fire elemental breath described in Practice #2 above. Concentrate on a red light at the bottom of the spine, salmon light in the areas around the navel, orange in the solar plexus, gold in the heart, green in the throat, blue in the eyes, indigo in the third eye, and colorless diamond-like light above the crown. Your body is a rainbow of light, and this intensifies as you concentrate upon it. After a few minutes, imagine a further rainbow that begins up in the crown center. Imagine the whole spectrum of light, smaller and more subtle, extending upwards, becoming more and more transparent. Again after a few minutes, visualize yet another rainbow above the last, on and on upwards in realms of light.

2. *By the power of our creative glance, we are able to begin to see life in the same way as the great prophets and teachers who came to guide humanity. Honor the truth that the world around us needs our light and intention. This is truly a practice of "concentration with improvement"—never a denial of the problems in front of us, but a way of finding the ultimate remedy for our situation. No longer succumbing to cold facts and sclerosed viewpoints, we can access the depths of the creative imagination and infuse this life with the light that is so needed. By shining this light, we make possibilities clear. Holding a vision of what could be, we are able to affirm and cultivate the beauty of what actually is, the beauty so often veiled by strife, agitation, doubt and despondency.*

3. *From the heights of meditation, open your eyes and again feel that they are like search lamps, illuminating the field of your vision. Instead of focusing on discrete objects, you are looking into an ocean of light. Without focusing on any objects or people, and with your glance not fixed on any object, infuse this instant of time with light, freshness and possibility. Realize that this illumination will eventually allow you to recognize the way that potential seeks to unfold, called in the Sufi tradition the "Divine Intention."*

4. *Finally, realize that the quality of your glance is what makes the life in front of you flourish. Smile with the light and power of your heart on this world, where all human beings and situations are so in need of the light of inspiration, vision and love. Your radiant being is a transformative power.*

Where'er you tread the blushing flowers
shall rise,
And all things flourish where
you turn your eyes.[129]

Practice #24: Fruitfulness

If life were for spirituality alone, the soul
had better not have been born on earth,
for the soul in its nature is spiritual. The
whole creation is purposed for something greater than goodness or even
spirituality, and that is fruitfulness. If there is any goal, it is fruitfulness.
There comes a time in the life of the fruitful souls when every moment
bears a new fruit.[130]

There is a Chinese image of "philosophers carrying peaches" on their shoulders, symbolic of the ultimate object of life as being fruitfulness. For fruitfulness in nature, a plant must be very healthy, well nourished and complete. For the entire process of unfolding, the plant takes what it needs of soil, water, light and air. Similarly, for our fruitfulness in the world, we must first be able to benefit our own life. Accomplishing this, we may then turn our attention to helping, to serving life. The culmination of fruitfulness will be when, by the continuing cultivation of our beings, our lives become fruitful for our world and also for ourselves.

1. To begin this practice, feel yourself to be like a tree, somewhere
in its process of growth towards fruitfulness. Realize that all
of your life experience, seemingly favorable or unfavorable, has
somehow served to make you more fruitful. Every difficulty, ev-
ery struggle is the work of cultivation, bringing your being out
of the dark earth into full blossom. Feel the taste of fruitfulness
within the body, and imagine the flavor and fruitfulness of your-
self as a fully ripened human being.

2. Experience the qualities that pour out from you. You may carry
energies that are like bubbling streams and radiant golden fields.
Your being may radiate understanding, compassion, generosity,

[129] Alexander Pope, *Poetical Works* (London: W.P. Nimmo, 1876), p. 218.

[130] Hazrat Inayat, Khan, *The Sufi Message of Hazrat Inayat Khan*, Vol. XIII: The Gathas (Geneva, International Sufi Movement, 1982), p. 105.

love, peace, joy, the union of heaven and earth. Recognize your capacity to find satisfaction in your own life and to bring the fruit of your life to others. Meditate on these thoughts of Sufi Saint Muinuddin Chishti: "Be as magnanimous as the river, kind as the sun and humble as the earth." You may wish to conclude with this prayer of Hazrat Inayat Khan: "Make my life fruitful and joy-giving in every direction."

Epilogue:
An Elixir For Humanity

And Thy Lord taught the Bee
to build its cells in hills,
on trees and in human habitations;
then to eat of all
the produce of the earth,
and find with skill and humility the
spacious paths of the Lord;
there issues from within their bodies
a drink of varying colors,
wherein is healing for humanity;
verily in this is a Sign
for those who give thought.

—Qur'an Sura 16, Verses 68-70

OUR EARTH AND ITS INHABITANTS ARE SUFFERING. The natural world is being ravaged by the presence and the activities of human beings. The degree of destruction and suffering is almost unbearable to contemplate.

But contemplate we must. While reports vary, between ten and one hundred species of living beings—animals and plants—become extinct each day. The rate of deforestation and rapid disappearance of tropical rainforests is staggering. A recent UNICEF report states that over one billion children, half of the world's child population, are actually denied a childhood. Some 640 million children lack adequate shelter; 400 million have no access to safe drinking water; 150 million are malnourished; 270 million lack health care amenities and 140 million— mostly girls— have never been to school.

In this book we have emphasized that realizing our deepest identity and finding the true purpose of our life is paramount to alleviating the problems around us. This is not the exclusive answer to these crises, but it is both a prerequisite and a pathway to wise and enduring solutions. Instead of identifying culprits and enemies, instead of grand plans for social reform, we must begin by realizing who we are, and the truth that the outside world reflects something of our inner condition. Clarifying and cultivating our hearts will bring harmony, and yield a discerning light which can be cast both within and on the life around us. By this light we can best cultivate all the richness and potentialities that we are given, experiencing most tangibly the marriage of heaven and earth, of inner and outer universes.

The above verses of the Qur'an on the bee summarize the whole spiritual journey and its fulfillment. We can learn a great deal from the bee, who naturally brings forth a nectar that is healing for all. There are no claims, no religions, no particular enemies identified by the bee, only an alignment with nature's ways and the precious creature's own unique purpose in this life.

The bee truly lives naturally—it eats of the wide variety of produce of the earth, it builds houses and, most importantly, it skillfully finds the "spacious pathways" of its Lord. The bee teaches us to find our natural self, not a coercive and restricted way of life, but an ease, a spaciousness, an acceptance of our work in the world and our unique way of unfolding.

Of course we could say that the human being's reality is much more complex than that of the bee. There is more than instinct involved in our journeying, and the greater complexity adds greater challenges. What comes to the bee by pure instinct, we have to recapture, and our journey has many more turns and many more obstacles to surmount, requiring of us more wisdom and creativity.

For example, we need to cultivate our capacities for concentration and diligence, and ultimately apply these to the problems of the life around us. But we must also embrace a radical opening of consciousness—opening to help coming from unseen directions and to the emergence of new possibilities—that will guide us towards the future.

The universe has its own pathways, its own bent in unfolding. The more we touch our natural being, the more we are familiar with this bent. When we are oriented towards service, a link exists between our particular way of meeting life and what is literally the "thinking of the Universe" emerging to meet the challenges of this world.

The more we are willing to do the "work" we have described here, the more opportunities we are given to become, like the bee, a healing elixir for the world around us. Indeed we will discover, as Chogyam Trungpa taught, that we become like shock absorbers in the world of agitation in which we find ourselves. This is the way that the confusion, agitation and disharmony around us are transformed into a healing nectar.

Inayat Khan taught the importance of recognizing life's alchemy, of recognizing, in the brief moments of our lives, the birthing of a new universe. This birth, with its inevitable pains and stretching, takes place right in the nitty gritty, in the drama of our everyday existence. This is the ever "new creation" that we have the magnificent opportunity to gaze upon and share in, "on the horizon and inside of ourselves."

Amidst great intensity, we can realize most clearly this powerful yet simple alchemy that is emerging in our lives. The universe does ask us, continually, to observe, to "learn from the bee," to bring forth the beauty and essence of life in our being. Our fruitfulness will not only benefit others but be our own fulfillment as well:

> It takes all the patience one has to arrive at this realization, but it is for this: There is a great treasure of blessing within oneself and there is a vast treasure of blessing outside oneself, and when one has become able to find out the treasure one has within oneself and to exploit the treasure which is outside oneself, and when there is an exchange between one's own treasure and the treasure outside, then one's life has borne the fruit for which the soul was born.[131]

Our satisfaction is before us, and waits most patiently to be recognized, appreciated and fully embraced. It is linked to being of service, and to answering the cry of suffering all around us, in people and in our natural world. Let us work actively and open to what is possible, aligning to the life energy and wisdom that are arising continually. Again we invoke the passionate call of Nikos Kazantzakis, reflecting deeply on the truth of his challenging words:

> Everything you do reverberates through a thousand destinies. As you walk, you cut open and create the riverbed into which the stream of your descendants shall enter and flow....

> We are one. From the blind worm in the depths of the ocean to the endless arena of the Galaxy, only one person struggles and is imperiled: you. And within your small and earthen breast only one thing struggles and is imperiled: the Universe.[132]

The Emerald Earth is right here, existing in the fullness of our intention. It is not found in an enchanted land or esoteric ritual. We *can* be guided by Creative Beauty, understanding what is ever being asked

[131] Hazrat Inayat, Khan, *The Sufi Message of Hazrat Inayat Khan*, Vol. XIII: The Gathas (Geneva, International Sufi Movement, 1982), p. 106.

[132] Nikos Kazantzakis, *The Saviors of God*, trans. Kimon Friar (New York: Simon and Schuster, 1960), p. 105.

of us. Our attuned and enlightened hearts can see, can read the guidance within the sacred manuscript of nature, and can serve the power of the natural world to restore Herself. When we are properly aligned to this power, we will recognize inspiration and help from sources Unseen, and will ourselves bring to awareness the Sacred Presence and Loving Mystery that has been guiding us since our first breath.

In the most peaceful and stabilizing way, the great tradition of Zen helps us gradually assimilate the truth that both shatters us and makes us free. Zen Master Dogen uses the bright star, the young pine tree or the mountain to remind us of life's mystery and prom-ise. He speaks of "mountains walking," and of how the great ancient mountains have been "walking" since beginningless time. The mountains are moun-tains, truly, but they are also a mirror for the reality of our own being. We *are* the moun-tains, and this walking, this gradual journeying, is familiar. We are inseparable from the greatest mystery, the very Life  of this universe and of all universes. We are Sophia, on the return leg of a long and ancient journey, here to realize in ourselves the wisdom and splendor behind creation, and to witness the unveiling of these as beauty and intelligence on an Emerald Earth.

Ironically, by being aware of the dreamlike aspect of our exis-tence, we are in a position to best revere our sacred Earth, and to find concrete solutions to the problems we face. Feeling our connection with mountains and flowing waters, with the light and air that purify and vitalize us, we have a better sense of those attitudes and actions which are in harmony with Nature. We also become acutely aware of all that is not part of such harmony and that stands in opposition to Nature's ways of expressing Her beauty.

May we truly learn from the bee, bringing forth a healing elixir from our bodies, hearts and souls. May we allow Creative Beauty, ever present, to be our reference point in this world. May we realize, even in the most difficult of times, the vital importance of continually orienting ourselves on the spiritual path, affirming beauty and gaining trust in the mercy and beneficence of life. May we be nourished by meditation, continually receiving new life energy and, in turn, offering this to all those around us. May we ever be tuned to a resonant and divine pitch, aware of the splendor of the heavens that is always seeking expression. May we continually devote ourselves to the care and cultivation of this precious life, and may we fully realize that a light-filled Emerald Earth is awakening and unfolding in each moment. May we become beacons of light and life, and thereby offer the bread and wine of love and the soothing balm of peace to each other and to all of life.

Till the end of time, matter will always remain young, exuberant, sparkling, newborn for those who are willing.[133]

---

[133] Teilhard DeChardin, *The Hymn of the Universe.* (New York: Harper and Row, 1981), p.64.

A Prayer for Peace

Send Thy Peace Oh Lord,
Which is Perfect and Everlasting
That Our Souls May Radiate Peace.
Send Thy Peace, Oh Lord,
That We May Think, Act and Speak Harmoniously.
Send Thy Peace, Oh Lord,
That We May Be Contented And Thankful
For Thy Bountiful Gifts.
Send Thy Peace, Oh Lord,
That Amidst Our Worldly Strife
We May Enjoy Thy Bliss.
Send Thy Peace, Oh Lord,
That We May Endure All, Tolerate All,
In The Thought of Thy Grace And Mercy.
Send Thy Peace, Oh Lord,
That Our Lives May Become A Divine Vision,
And In Thy Light, All Darkness May Vanish.
Send Thy Peace, Oh Lord, Our Father and Mother
That We, Thy Children On Earth,
May All Unite, In One Family. Amen

—Hazrat Inayat Khan

About the Authors

Felicia Norton and Charles Smith serve as senior teachers and meditation retreat guides within the Sufi Order International (www.sufiorder.org) and Ziraat (www.ziraat.org).

Felicia is the leader of the Ziraat Activity of the Sufi Order in North America. She is a classically trained dancer, performing internationally, and teaches at the United Nations School and the Educational Alliance in New York City.

Charles teaches organization theory, leadership skills and group dynamics at Hofstra University, and writes on applications of Sufi perspectives to decision making, creativity and leadership. He is a trustee of the Sufi Order International.

Felicia and Charles are married and live in New York City, also studying within the Nur Ashki Jerrahi Sufi tradition and the Kagyu lineage of Tibetan Buddhism. Together the authors founded the Light of Guidance Center for Sufi Studies in New York City and guide workshops and retreats internationally on the central practices found in *An Emerald Earth*.

Contact information and a schedule of the authors' upcoming programs can be found at www.anemeraldearth.org.

About Ziraat

The Ziraat Activity within the Sufi Order International connects the cultivation of the heart and soul with our responsibility of honoring and serving the sacred in all of life.

The word "ziraat" means agriculture in Persian. The primitive root "zara," found in the Semitic languages, means "to sow, disseminate, plant, fructify, and to conceive seed."

Ziraat uses the dynamic symbols of agriculture and their correspondences to reveal the alchemy of the spiritual path. It emphasizes fruitfulness and service to all of life as the ultimate harvest of the spiritual journey.

For more information on Ziraat see www.ziraat.org.